UKRAINE

NATURE
TRADITIONS
CULTURE

Baltia Druk
Publishers

UKRAINE

The National Emblem of Ukraine is the State symbol of Ukraine.
The principal element of the Great State Emblem of Ukraine
is the Symbol of the Princely State of Volodymyr the Great
(little State Emblem of Ukraine)

Ukraine is administratively divided into 24 Oblasts,
2 cities of republican subordination (Kyiv, Sevastopol),
and the Autonomous Republic of the Crimea.
Kyiv is the capital of Ukraine

The National Flag of Ukraine
is a State symbol of Ukraine.
This is a banner of two equidimensional horizontal
blue and yellow strips

СОФІЯ

GENERAL INFORMATION

GEOGRAPHY

Ukraine is a State situated in the south of Eastern Europe. By its territory Ukraine holds the first place among European countries. Within the present-day borders Ukraine covers an area of 603,700 sq. km.

The territory of Ukraine is mostly plains with individual hills rising up to 300 m above sea level. The Carpathian Mountains (the peak being Mount Hoverla — 2,061 m high, the highest in the country) are situated in the west of Ukraine.

The Crimean Mountains are situated on the southern coast of the Crimea (Mount Roman Kosh — 1,545 m high). The lowest point of Ukraine is to be found on the bottom of the Black Sea (2,245 m).

Almost all the inland rivers of Ukraine flow to the south and belong to the basins of the Black Sea and the Sea of Azov. There are almost 4 thousand rivers in Ukraine, each of them being more than 10 km long. The largest of them are: the Dnipro in the center of the country (total length being 2,201 km, 981 km within the borders of Ukraine), the Siversky Dinets (total length — 1,053 km; within Ukraine's borders 672 km) in the east, the Pivdenny Buh (806 km long) and the Dnister (1,362 km long) in the west, and the Danube (2,850 km long, 174 km within Ukraine) in the south. The only river running to the north is the Zakhidny Buh (834 km long, 401 km within Ukraine) flowing into the Vistula in the territory of Poland.

CLIMATE

The territory of Ukraine is situated mainly in the temperate continental zone, and only the southern coast of the Crimea is to be found in subtropical zone. The average temperature in January is from –8°C in the east and the north, up to +2°C in the south; the average temperature in July is from +17°C in the west and the north, up to +25°C in the south.

Precipitation quantity gradually decreases from the north to the south: approximately 1,500 mm per year in the Carpathians, and less that 300 mm on the Black Sea coast.

THE MAJOR CITIES

Kyiv 2,611 thousand
Kharkiv 1,470 thousand
Dnipropetrovsk 1,065 thousand
Odesa 1,029 thousand
Donetsk 1,016 thousand
Zaporizhia 815 thousand
Lviv 733 thousand.

POPULATION

The population of Ukraine is 48,457 thousand (census of 2001). By this index Ukraine is the fifth largest country in Europe after FRG, Italy, Great Britain and France, and 22nd in the world. Urban population makes up 67%. The average density of population is 81 per 1 sq. km. Sex structure: male — 46%; female — 54%. Life expectancy — 66 years.

ETHNIC MAKE-UP

Representatives of almost 130 nationalities inhabit the territory of Ukraine.

Ukrainians 78%
Russians 17%
Belarussians 0,6%
Moldavians 0,5%
Crimean Tatars 0,5%
Bulgarians 0,4%
Poles 0,3%
Hungarians 0,3%
Romanians 0,3%
Greeks 0,2%
Jews 0,2%
Others 1,7%

GOVERNMENT INSTITUTIONS

The foundations of the State system are determined by the Constitution of Ukraine.
Ukraine is a republic.
President is the head of the State.
Prime minister is the head of the government.
Verkhovna Rada (Supreme Council) is the highest legislative body.

RELIGION

Orthodox believers 72%
Greek-Catholics 18%
Protestants 5%
Catholics 4%
Others 1%
Monetary unit is hryvnia = 100 kopecks
National holiday — August 24 (Independence Day)
Zone time: +2 hours to Greenwich.
State language — Ukrainian.

1
The row

2
Geographical column near the Central Post Office in Kyiv

HISTORICAL EVENTS

860–882 The reign of Kyivan Prince *Askold*, first mentioned in Byzantine sources.

988 The baptism of Rus by Kyivan Prince *Volodymyr Sviatoslavych*.

1015–1016 Conclusion of the first legal code *Ruska Pravda*.

1017–1037 Construction of St. Sophia Cathedral and the Golden Gate in Kyiv.

1239–1240 The Mongol invasion. *Batu* Khan conquers Chernihiv and Kyiv.

1253 Envoys of Pope Innocent IV crown Galician Prince *Danylo Romanovych* as “the king of Rus”.

1343–1362 Division of Ukrainian lands between Polish kingdom and the grand Lithuanian duchy.

1550s Foundation of *Zaporozhian Sich* on *Mala Khortytsia* Island on the Dnipro River.

1569 Polish kingdom and the grand Lithuanian duchy unite into the federative State *Rzeczpospolita*.

1574 Ivan Fedorov founded the first Ukrainian printing-house in Lviv.

1581 Publication of the first printed Bible in the Old Church Slavonic language.

1596 Conclusion of the union between the Roman Catholic and Orthodox Churches at the council in *Berest*. Foundation of the *Uniate* (Greek-Catholic) Church.

1648 Beginning of the liberation war under the leadership of *Bohdan Khmelnytsky*; foundation of the Ukrainian Cossack State (*Hetmanate*).

1654 Decision of *Pereyaslav Rada* (Council) to adopt protectorate of the Russian czar by the Cossack State.

1658–1686 Polish-Russian war that ended in the division of the Ukrainian territory between Russia and *Rzeczpospolita*.

1772–1795 Collapse of *Rzeczpospolita* and transference of Ukraine’s western regions to the Austrian Empire, and central and eastern regions to the Russian Empire.

1775 Manifesto of Catherine II about liquidation of *Zaporozhian Sich*.

1784 Lviv Jesuit *Collegium* received the status of the first university in Ukrainian lands.

1805–1834 Opening of universities in Kharkiv (1805) and Kyiv (1834).

1845–1846 Foundation of *Cyrill-and-Methodius Brotherhood*, a cultural and educational Christian-democratic organization.

1848 Abolition of serfdom in Austro-Hungary.

1848–1906 Issue of the first Ukrainian newspapers in Lviv and Kyiv.

1860–1900 National cultural organizations work in Petersburg and Kyiv.

1861 Abolition of serfdom in the Russian Empire.

1866 Putting into operation of the first railways in the Ukrainian territories of Russia and Austro-Hungary.

1917 The overthrow of Russian autocracy; declaration of two independent Ukrainian States — Ukrainian People's Republic with capital city in Kyiv, and Ukrainian Soviet Socialist Republic with capital in *Kharkiv*.

1918–1921 A change of governments, Civil War and Russian-Ukrainian and Polish-Ukrainian wars in the territory of Ukraine; defeat of the Ukrainian national movement.

1922 Formation of the Union of Soviet Socialist Republics (USSR) with the Ukrainian Soviet Socialist Republic as part of it.

1929–1933 Liquidation of private land property and formation of collective farms, mass deportation of rural population to the north of Russia, organization of artificial famine in Ukrainian countryside — Famine of 1932–1933.

1939 The outbreak of World War II; reunification of Eastern and Western Ukraine as a result of occupation of Western Ukraine by the Soviet troops; occupation of Carpathian Ukraine by Hungarian army.

1941 The outbreak of the Great Patriotic War on the territory of the Soviet Union; occupation of Ukraine by Nazi Germany.

1945 The USSR gained victory in the Great Patriotic War; the end of World War II; inclusion of western Ukrainian lands, *Bukovyna* and Carpathian Ukraine in the Ukrainian Soviet Socialist Republic.

1954 Crimea is removed from the Russian Federation and transferred to Ukraine.

1956–1964 Relaxation of totalitarian regime during Mykyta Khruschev (the so-called "thaw").

1965–1977 Political repressions, the end of political "thaw," the growth of dissident movement among the intellectuals; organization in 1976 of Ukrainian Helsinki Group.

3
The Baptism of Kyivites by Prince Volodymyr.
Fresco by V. Vasnetsov in St. Volodymyr's Cathedral

1990 *Verkhovna Rada* of the Ukrainian SSR approves Declaration on the State Sovereignty of Ukraine.

1991 *Verkhovna Rada* of the Ukrainian SSR approves Act of Declaration of Independence of Ukraine.

1996 *Verkhovna Rada* adopted Constitution of Ukraine; introduction of the national currency — *hryvnia*.

2004 *Pomarancheva* (Orange) Revolution and election of Viktor *Yuschenko* President of Ukraine.

2004 Ukrainian singer Ruslana came out winner of the Eurovision song contest which proved that Ukrainian pop-music is in keeping with world standards.

2010 Election of Viktor *Yanukovych* President of Ukraine.

2012 Kyiv will be one of the cities hosting UEFA's EURO Football Championship.

NATURE

Ukrainian nature is shrouded in a special poetic coloring. There is nothing motley or sharp about it, in contrast it is caressing and attractive. Mild climate, the generous sun, rich verdure, the diversity of landscapes have long been fascinating travelers, poets and artists. The French novelist Honoré de Balzac called Ukraine "the kingdom of flowers and verdure."

According to old myths Ukraine is one of the finest lands in the world where rivers flow like those of milk and honey, where song of the birds flows over the fields and woods, where earthly and heavenly miracles happen at once. There are three main nature zones in Ukraine: forest, forest-steppe and steppe zones. There inimitable landscapes are like variations of the same musical theme.

Forest zone — Ukrainian Polissia — occupies northern Ukraine (25% of its total territory). In the west Polissia adjoins Volyn

area. Dark meadows, pine forests, silvery rivers and nature itself seem to embroider fascinating landscapes of multicolor threads. Once this territory was covered with glacier. Glacial epoch left expressive traces of itself. Wherever you cast a glance you will see a swamped plain. Here and there slightly sloping hills rise over impassible bogs. Shallow reservoirs, the only fresh water lakes in Ukraine, lie between them. Stone boulders are scattered everywhere. Raised sandy places are covered with woods.

5
The Chinese bridge in the park Oleksandria

6–7
Crimean landscapes

8
Winter landscape

9
Autumn leaf fall

Deep rivers flow unhurriedly down the broad soggy valleys: the Prypiat River in the west, and the Desna River in the east.

Oaks, pine-trees, hornbeams, alder-trees and birches are growing in forests. Here you may come across elks, roes, wild boars, hares, foxes, martens, beavers, minks, badgers, ermines and stoats, wolves, brown bears, forest cats, lynxes, musk-rats and other animals. Rare species of birds build their nests in wild forests: wood, black and hazel grouses, thrushes, swans, cranes and storks. Snakes are creeping among thick bushes. Miriad of insects are swarming over the bogs. The Chornobyl disaster inflicted a crippling blow on Polissia nature, having contaminated a considerable territory with radionuclids.

Forest-steppe zone (33% of the country's area) stretches across the central part of Ukraine — 1,100 km long and up to 140 km wide. This strip of land has the most favorable conditions for life. The most fertile chernozem soils are concentrated in this area. Most of the forest-steppe zone is occupied by arable land, the rest is populated. Oak, hornbeam, sycamore and pine-tree prevail in the forests. The animal kingdom is represented by hares, foxes, roes, elks and deer.

The nature of Ukrainian forest-steppe is unrivaled regarding its beauty. The steppe motley grass is scarcely swaying in the breeze, pensive pussy-willows bend their twigs to the lakes, mighty oaks exchange words with poplars, the depth of steep-sloped gullies covered with woods and shrubs is really enchanting, wood-covered river banks and light-winged cloudlets are reflected in the waters of fast-flowing rivers. And the blue cupola of the sky spreads out far and wide over the fire-yellow fields of ripe wheat.

This unification of blue and yellow — the color of the sky and the color of the earth lit by the sun — is an integral part of Ukrainian national psychology and has found its reflection in the colors of the national flag.

A characteristic feature of the Ukrainian forest-steppe scenery is the asymmetry of river valleys and interriver expanses. The right bank — high, steep, cut with gullies, and rocky in some places — falls down to the river like a steep slope. Flood plains with bogs, old riverbeds and meadows lie on the left bank. Further from the river the bank becomes steeper and gradually turns into an interriver range that again descends headlong to the neighboring river. Relief drops create new and new pictures, and the line of horizon disappears in the transparent air like an optical illusion.

Steppe zone (39% of the country's area) is situated in the south of Ukraine, stretching out as a tract of land which is up to 1,000 km long and more than 500 km wide. Almost over the whole of its stretch it is a vast flat plain. The monotony of the scenery is diversified by solitary gullies, lakes and shallow hollows that fill with water in spring, and get covered with lush grass in summer. At this time the steppe turns into a variegated flower garden spreading wonderful scents in the air. Small woods and bushes grow in damp gullies (oak, maple, ash, linden, hawthorn, thorn bush, wild rose).

10–11
Carpathian suite

Due to the highly productive chernozem soils Ukrainian steppe zone is one of the biggest regions in the world for growing high-quality varieties of wheat, sunflower, grapes, melons and gourds.

In summer the steppe suffers from lack of water. The small steppe rivers partially or fully dry up. Their exhausted currents cannot fight the sea and form coastal salines. The quiet reaches of the salines are in contrast with the spits cutting the water surface.

Unique salines are to be found in the Crimean steppes. For many centuries carters' caravans delivered salt to Ukraine from there.

In Aigulsk Lake the salt layer is up to 15 meters thick, and salt saturation is about 32% in summer.

Unique nature creations — mud volcanoes — can be seen in Kerch Peninsula.

The Carpathian and Crimean Mountains are situated in the west and south of Ukraine respectively. The Carpathian Mountains occupy the territory of seven countries: Austria, the Czech Republic, Slovakia, Poland, Hungary, Romania and Ukraine, covering the total area of 209 thousand sq. km. Twenty four thousand sq. km of this territory (11.5%) fall on Ukraine. The highest point of the Ukrainian Carpathians is Mount Hoverla (2,061 m high). The top of Hoverla is a particular symbol of Ukraine's grandeur and pride. The volcanic activity of the Carpathians ceased long ago, but the mountains remain seismically active even today.

Mountain landscapes are really fantastic. The bow-shaped mountain ranges alternate with narrow valleys that sometimes look like canyons. Waterfalls carve their way through the rocky precipices. The blue eyes of the deep lakes are looking into the boundless sky. The mountain slopes are covered with fir trees, beeches, oaks and hornbeams. The woods are rich in herbs, mushrooms, fruit and berries. The animals living in there are represented by bears, wolves, lynxes, martens, deer, roes, wild boars, squirrels and hares. Closer to the summits the woods pass into alpine meadows that serve as pastureland for domestic animals in summer.

12
Trembitas sound

13–16
From the life of insects

The Carpathians are fascinating at any season of the year. The rich ethnographic coloring of landscape, small tidy houses, the soft contours of the mountains, the emerald-blue waves of coniferous woods and mountain meadows and the sparkling snow of mountain-skiing routs cannot but attract tourists, mountaineers and holiday-makers.

The Crimean mountain region is situated in the south-east of the Crimean Peninsula. It consists of three parallel ridges stretching for 180 km in length and 60 km in width. In contrast with the Carpathians the process of mountain-formation in the Crimea has not finished: the mountains and the adjoining maritime area of the Black Sea are a highly seismic region where earthquakes are a periodical occurrence.

The Crimean mountains are not high — from 200 to 1,500 meters. The highest peak is Mount Roman-Kosh (1,545 m). The mountain slopes are covered with oak, beech and pine forests; the treeless mountain pastures (yailas) are covered with the steppe vegetation. Animal population is represented by deer, badgers, foxes, wild boars, black gryphons, peregrin falcons, Balkan snakes and Ukrainian boas.

Small swift rivers are running down the narrow valleys and deep ravines. In summer almost all of them dry up. Descending steeply to the sea the mountains form a forbidding stone conglomeration.

To the east of Baidarsky Gate the mountains are separated from the sea by a flat 12 km-wide beech. This is the famous Crimean Riviera with marvelous bays, Mediterranean climate and evergreen plants (cypress, magnolia, myrtle, laurel). The mountain Crimea enjoys wide popularity with holiday makers.

Ukraine is a naval power. In the south it is washed by the Black Sea and the Sea of Azov. Its maritime regions are generally known as a place of rest and medical treatment.

The Black Sea occupies an area of 422 sq. km, its seashore stretch within the borders of Ukraine is 1,560 km long. In the north-west it is not deep (about 100 m). In the rest of its territory it is 2,000 meters deep and more. The deepest cavity (2,245 m) lies in front of Yalta. There are many bays suitable for moorings. The biggest seaports of Ukraine are situated on the Black Sea coast: Odesa, Illichivsk, Yuzhny, Mykolaiv, Kherson, Sevastopol, Feodosia and Kerch.

In summer water temperature reaches 25 °C. 180 species of fish and 260 kinds of sea weeds inhabit the Black Sea. The accumulation of the iodine containing red sea weeds near the seashore of Ukraine is the richest in the world. High percentage of hydrogen sulphide at the depth of 150–200 meters makes any kind of organic life in the Black Sea impossible. The Straits of Kerch (40 km long, 4–36 km wide) join the Black Sea and the Sea of Azov.

The Sea of Azov (39 thousand sq. km, 360 km long within the borders of Ukraine) is shallow (5–10 meters), the deepest place being 15 meters in the south. In summer the sea waters warm up to 30 oC and freeze in winter. Fish from the Black Sea come to the Sea of Azov to spawn. Industrial fishing is practiced here for khamsa, pike-perch, beluga, herring, bullhead, sea-roach and flat-fish. The major seaports are Berdiansk and Mariupol.

The seashore is cut by numerous bow-shaped spits isolating bays and coastal lakes. Arabatska Strilka, the largest spit (115 km long, 7 km wide), separates the salt lake Sivash (2,870 sq. km) from the Sea of Azov. Life is impossible in Sivash because its waters are saturated with iodine salts.

The Dnipro River — the "sacred current" — has a devout meaning for Ukraine. The life of the Ukrainian people has been linked with it from time immemorial. It is the axis of Ukraine. It flows through the middle of Ukraine from the north to the south, cutting across all of its nature zones and connecting them to the sea. The Dnipro is 981 km long in the territory of Ukraine.

The Ukrainian people have held their sacred river in high respect since olden days. It is linked with the legend of the foundation of Kyiv, with old stories about the baptism of Ukraine-Rus, about the wars of our ancestors against numerous enemies. The respectful folklore epithet Slavuta (distinguished, eminent) was mentioned in old written sources, oral tradition, ballads and songs.

T. Shevchenko's Testament and the funeral of the poet on Chernecha Hill overlooking the Dnipro determined the ever-living tradition of revering the Dnipro as an object of worship.

17
Reflection

18–20
In the mountains

PARKS AND RESERVES

Natural landscapes of Ukraine have been considerably changed by the economic activity of man. Thus, for instance, Ukraine exceeds Germany, France, Italy, the USA and Japan by such an index as the ratio of arable land to the total area of agricultural lands. For this reason, and because of scanty forests (13% of the whole territory) Ukraine cannot create numerous and spacious reserves. The protected area makes up only 4% of its territory.

Shatsky National Nature Park was founded in 1986 in a picturesque corner of Volyn Polissia. One fifth of the park's territory is occupied by the famous Shatsky lakes (more than 30 in number). Water in them is clean and drinking. More than 28 species of fish live in the lakes. Shatsky lakes is the only place in Ukraine where eels are bred and fished (natural habitat being the Sargasso Sea). There are holiday homes, sanatoriums, sport and children's camps on the lakesides. Special places are allocated for parking lots and fishing. A visit to the park leaves an unforgettable impression of the picturesque scenery, clear air, and hospitality of the local population.

In the boggy area of Volyn Polissia the *Rivnensky Nature Reserve* was founded in 1999. It represents all types of Polissia swamps. The largest peatbog in Ukraine — *Kremyiane* — is to be found in the territory of the Reserve. The maximum thickness of the peat layer there exceeds five meters.

The *Polissia Nature Reserve* founded in 1968 is situated in the central Polissia, in the upper reaches of the Ubort River. A considerable part of it is covered with swamps and overgrown with lichen and green moss. Vast areas are covered with bilberries, cowberries, and fern. The fauna of the reserve is represented by 40 species of animals. Otters and beavers, rare in Ukraine, live near the river banks, lynxes are to be found in the depths of the forest, and black storks and wood-grouses build their nests there.

The *Desna-Starohuty National Nature Park* was laid out in 1999 in eastern Polissia (Novhorod Siverske Polissia). The local meadows and swamps are inhabited by beavers, otters and ermines.

The *Nature Reserve Roztochia* occupies a small territory in the extreme west of the Ukrainian forest-steppe zone. Its name (lit. "Spilling") derives from its location at the major European watershed where many rivers spring from. Forest, water, meadow and swamp ecologic systems of the resere are really unique. Ther are trees here that are more than a hundred years old. Amphibians and reptiles are widespread in the reserve.

The narrow and hilly range *Tovtry* can be clearly seen in the relief of Podillia Hills. The woody areas there are rich in melliferous herbs, hence the name of the *Nature Reserve Medobory* (Honey taking) founded in 1990. It contains old oak-groves, beech woods and a hornbeam forest with more than a thousand species of plants. The reserve is inhabited by hare, fox, roe, elk and deer.

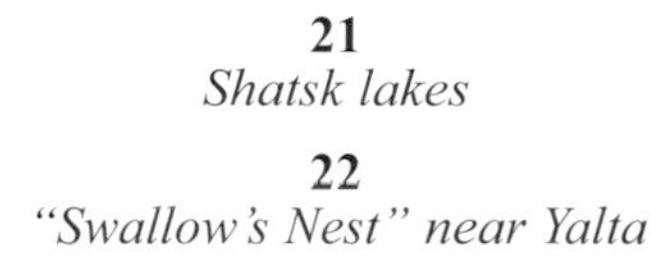

21
Shatsk lakes

22
"Swallow's Nest" near Yalta

Laid out in 1996 in the territory of Khmelnytsky and neighboring Oblasts the *National Nature Park "Podillia Tovtry"* occupies the largest area in Ukraine — 261.3 thousand hectares. The valley of the River Dnistro with its tributaries on the left is a unique natural landmark. Cutting deeply into the limestone hills the rivers meander among the canyon-like slopes.

The park is particularly proud of the historical and cultural complexes of the old town of *Kamyianets-Podilsky*: the fortress, the Armenian church, the Franciscan and Dominican monasteries, the Roman-Catholic Cathedral with a Turkish minaret crowned with Christian Madonna.

There are different kinds of itineraries: pedestrian, mounted, by water, ski, motor-car, or bicycle. They envisage visiting the mountain *Bokotsky Monastery*, caves, parks, mineral springs, and forest dachas.

In the central part of the Dnipro reaches, along the right bank of the river, stretch Kaniv mountains. In the course of centuries these

territories organically united the history of nature and the people. The exposure of old geological epochs with the remains of extinct flora and fauna represent a unique natural monument. On the northern shady slopes there may happen relic plants of the glacial epoch. The local oak-grove put an end to the advancement of European hornbeam woods to the east. The *Kaniv Nature Reserve* had been functioning there since 1923. The unique relief, the inimitable beauty of landscapes, the biological diversity surviving in the center of the densely populated country cannot but attract numerous tourists.

Of all the reserves and preserves in Ukraine the most important one is the Chernecha (Taras') Hill in Kaniv where lie the remains of the great national poet Taras Shevchenko. Annually this place is visited by more than 300 thousand tourists.

23–26
Dendropark Oleksandria

The *Dendrologic Park "Aleksandria,"* built by the serfs in the late 18th century and named after its former owner, the Polish Countess Aleksandra Branicka, is situated in the town of Bila Tserkva, on the left bank of the River Ros. The landscapes in the park are organically united with numerous architectural structures — pavilions, pergolas, colonnades, and bridges with romantic names ("Ruins," "A Turkish Building," "Chinese Bridge," "The Column of Sorrow," "Echo"). More than 1,800 species of exotic trees and bushes are growing in the park.

The *Dendrologic Reserve "Sophiyivka"* in Uman was created to order of the Count S. Potocki and named in honor of his wife Sophia. The landscape-architectural park with numerous hydro-constructions (sluice made in the rock, grottoes, waterfalls, pools, lakes, an underground river) and works of park architecture and sculptures on antique subjects was laid out on the area of 150 hectares in the terrain of Kamianka.

The *Luhansk Nature Reserve* was founded in 1968. It is an original island of the remains of wild nature among the densely populated industrial area. In contains unique tracks of the feather-grass steppes, wooded valleys, a great colony of European marmots. In adjusting themselves to the scorched steppe verdure the marmots change their coloration to imitate the color of the earth, burrow holes in the ground to protect themselves from bad weather, heat and enemies.

A big natural hill (up to 200 m in diameter and 15 m high) — *Kamiana Mohyla* (Stone Burial Mound) — is situated in the flood plain of the River Molochna near the Sea of Azov. It is one of the oldest sanctuaries and treasuries of knowledge in the world. Over millenniums *Kamiana Mohyla* was a place of religious ceremonies. The caves, grottoes and sheds have preserved pictures that, according to some scholars, are the oldest chronicle of the planet.

The *Dnipro-Orilsky Nature Reserve* is to be found in the middle reaches of the Dnipto. Research is being carried out there into flora and fauna under conditions of high environmental contamination. The Dnipro River once sung of in songs and legends today is taking in dead waters and the poisoned waste of industrial production. Long ago and today the broad river gave and continues to give life to nature and its destroyer — man.

There are oak-groves in the reserve where the song of birds — chaffinches, buntings, thrushes and tomtits — can be heard from early spring to late autumn. The gulls and sandpipers are roaming about the shallow waters. Hawks, kites and eagles are soaring in the sky, while the long-legged "fishers" — herons — are building their nests on the islands.

The *National Nature Reserve "Sviati Hory"* (Sacred Mountains) was founded in 1997. It occupies an area of 40 thousand hectares and spreads over the picturesque hills of the twisting river valley of the Siversky Dinets. Oak-groves, pine forests and various spe-

27–28
Picturesque corners in Sophiivka

cies of grass grow in the reserve. Nature has preserved necessary living conditions for many rare animals and birds.

The golden domes of the famous Sviatohirsk Dormition Monastery (17th–19th centuries) are glittering against the background of the white chalky slopes of the steep right bank of the river. Picturesque nature of the reserve attracts here numerous tourists and artists.

The oldest biosphere reserve *Askania Nova* is situated in the south of the steppe zone in Kherson Oblast. It is well known all over the world and was founded as a private botanical garden and zoo by the German colonist and great nature lover F. E. Valtz-Fein as long ago as the 1880s. In 1904 professor I. Ivanov worked at the reserve making interesting experiments on interbreeding of wild animals between themselves and with domesticated animals (aurochs and bison, aurochs-bison with cattle, zebra with horse). The area of the reserve is 33.3 thousand hectares one third of which is occupied by the steppe virgin soil. Half a thousand species of flowers are growing there, thirty of them are rare. Of great value is the botanical garden with its more than a hundred species

of acclimatized trees and bushes. The reserve had no equals in Ukraine as to the number of plant species (1960). Aboriginal fauna consists of deer, foxes, hares, marmots, adders, grass-snakes, steppe eagles. Scientists are carrying out work on acclimatizing some 50 species of animals and birds delivered from different corners of the world: bison, zebra, zebu, antelope, Przhevalsky horse, lama, moufflon, ostrich, flamingo, swan, pheasant. Most of them live in the open. Inimitable landscapes with herds of exotic animals, the cool of a man-made oasis among the steppe wilderness give birth to unforgettable impressions. Thousands of guests visit the *Askania* annually.

29–32
"Inhabitants" of Askania Nova reserve: Przhevalsky horse, marmot, deer, white swan

The *Chornomorsky* (Black Sea) *Biosphere Reserve* is situated in the territory of the neighboring Kherson and Mykolaiv Oblast, occupying an area of 89.1 thousand hectares. It consists of sea and continent sections, has been functioning since 1927, in 1985 it was given the status of a "biosphere reserve." This is the leading reserve by the number of birds. During season transmigration some 300 species of birds build their nests or rest in the reserve.

In 1998 the *Dunaisky Biospher Reserve* was founded in the lower reaches of the Danube. The reserve's territory mostly occupies the down-stream valley and delta of the Danube River. This is a real paradise for 4.5 thousand species of insects and 200 species of birds. The swamped plain cut with hundreds of branches and channels is covered with reeds and thickets that are the largest in Europe.

The settlement of Vylkove, called "Ukrainian Venice," is situated on the islands 18 km from the Sea of Azov. Original culture and traditions of the local population attract here tourists from all over

the world. The *Azov-Sivash National Nature Reserve* was founded in 1993 in the northern maritime regions of the Sea of Azov. Most of its territory (49 thousand hectares out of 57.4 thousand) is occupied by the waters of the Sea of Azov and the salt lake Sivash. It is the land of the steppe and alkali soil verdure. The routes of many birds of passage run through these lands.

33
Fountain "Night." Gurzuf. Crimea

34
Sculptural adornments of Sophiivka

35–36
The Southern coast of the Crimea

Carpathian Parks

The *Carpathian National Nature Park* is the largest nature park in the Carpathians. Its foundation lasted almost half a century and was completed in 1980. The park contains about 60% of the Ukrainian Carpathian flora. The master of the Carpathian Mountains is the brown bear.

Tourists are enchanted by the caves of Dovbush, the 12-meter high waterfall "The Surf" in Yaremcha, Hutsul wooden churches of the 16th–18th centuries.

The national nature park *Synevyr*, second in Ukraine by its territory, is situated in the majestic mountain-mass of Horhany at a height of 600–700 meters. The park has preserved virgin forests with rich flora and fauna.

There is trout in the reservoirs.

The name of the park derives from that of the Alpine lake personifying the fate of two legendary lovers — Syunia and Vyr. The lake looks like an eye looking at the blue sky: the water mirror is the eyeball, the islet is the apple of the eye, and the fir trees the eyelashes. Tourists from everywhere come here to admire this wonderful creation of nature.

The lake is situated at a height of 989 meters above sea level. Long ago a landslide dammed up a small stream there. The area of the lake is 4 hectares, the depth 24 meters. The constant temperature of the water is +11 °C.

Last century timber was rafted down the River Chorna from the mountains to the valley. There is the museum of timber rafting on the river bank, the only one in Europe, exhibiting implements of the courageous wood-cutters and rafters.

In 1968 the *Carpathian Biosphere Reserve* was set up in the Eastern Carpathians. It consists of five separate mountain forest tracts and the unique plain called the Dale of Narcissi. Wild virgin forests have preserved many rare and disappearing species of plants and animals.

In 1995 the *Vyzhnytsky National Nature Park* was founded in Bukovyna. The finery of the park is the precipices of the Dnister canyon, the silver reaches and noisy waterfall of the impetuous Prut and Cheremosh rivers, the emerald garments and the mysterious caves of the Khotyn and Chernivtsi hills. Beech and coniferous woods are inhabited by wild animals. "If God decided to spend his holidays on the Earth, he would choose Bukovyna," this old saying aptly characterizes this benevolent land.

The *National Nature Park Skoliv Beskydy* (founded 1999) spreads among thick forests and steep slopes. Centuries-old beech, fir tree and coniferous woods stand like an impenetrable wall. In 1965 ten aurochs were delivered to the park where they successfully live and breed.

37
The Carpathians in winter

38
The Carpathian museum of timber rafting

The representation of the trembita-player is the visiting-card of the park. This is the land of talented folk craftsmen whose original handicrafts (wood-carved articles, embroideries, carpets, necklaces, ceramics) are valued high far beyond the borders of the Carpathians.

The mysterious charms of the *Beskydy* attract numerous tourists. Here you can see the remnants of the unique fortress Tustan (9th–13th cent.) the 15-meter high walls of which were located on a rock 50 meters high. Detachments of Oleksa Dovbysh's brigands were active there in the first half of the 18th century.

The international reserve The *Eastern Carpathians* was founded in 1998 and included the nature protected areas of Ukraine, Poland and Slovakia.

Crimean Parks

The largest *Crimean Nature Reserve* is more than 90 years old. As long ago as 1913 the imperial reserve was founded in an inaccessible part of the Crimean Mountains. It was inhabited by wild animals delivered from the Caucasus, *Askania-Nova* and *Belovezhskaya Puscha reserves*. Today the reserve includes the mountain-forest section and Lebedyni (Swan) Islands in the Karkinit bay. Thirty species of rare animals are to be found in this territory.

The second largest is the *Yalta Mountain-Forest Nature Reserve* founded in 1973. It stretches along the southern coast of the Crimea for about 40 kilometers. Regarding the number of rare species of plants this reserve is really unique in Ukraine.

The *Karadag Nature Reserve* was founded in 1978 and occupies the north-eastern part of the Crimean Mountains. Its inimitable exotic beauty is caused to a large extent by its volcanic origin. Here you can see some 1,650 species of butterflies fluttering in the air, and rare reptiles in the motley grass.

In 1973 the *Nature Reserve "Cape Martian"* (240 hectares) was set up in the central part of the southern coast of the Crimea near Yalta. In fact it is a continuation of the Nikitsky Botanical Gardens. The area cut with gullies and deep ravines stretches from the mountain ridge to the sea. Typical Mediterranean plants that hibernate with open buds grow in the reserve. Reptiles inhabiting the area are represented by rare Crimean gecko, Balkan snake and leopard racer.

In 1998 the *Opuksky Nature Reserve* (1,592 hectares) was founded on the Kerch peninsula. Rare birds such as cormorant and peregrine falcon build their nests there.

In 1998 the *Kazantip Nature Reserve* (450 hectares) was organized on Cape Kazantip that is washed by the Sea of Azov. Its rarity gene pool contains 58 species of plants and animals.

39
Chersonesos ruins

40
Chersonesos ruins

41
Yalta embankment

42
Masandra park

ARCHITECTURE

In the course of their long history the Ukrainians proved to be a creative people sensitive to outside influence. Representatives of the oldest civilizations left their traces on the Ukrainian land. It may seem surprising but some burial mounds in Ukraine are older than the pyramids of Egypt. Four thousand years B.C. gigantic settlements existed in the territory of present-day Ukraine. The dimensions of *Bilsky* settlement of the 6th–4th century B. C. are really striking. Its famous contemporaries — Troy, Babylon and Athens — could easily go into its territory. Ruins of antique cities founded by Greek migrants have been preserved on the coast of the Black Sea and the Sea of Azov.

The ancestors of the Ukrainians had no problems with building materials, there was more than enough timber. A thousand and a half years ago, using axes, hammers, chisels and saws, without a nail, they raised towns, fortifications, palaces, modest huts and pagan temples.

During the old princely period (10th–13th centuries) stone building was widespread in Ukraine under the influence of Christian culture. Stones were used primarily for churches. The foundations were laid of rubble, the walls of thin bricks. The mixture of ground bricks and lime served as a mortar. The floors were paved with marble slabs.

The oldest types of stone churches were adopted from Byzantium. The Orthodox church differed from other structures in its drum — a spherical roof looking like a helmet. The number of the drums could be different, but in plan it was always cruciform. Inside the church was divided into naves separated by columns or arcades. It is interesting that Ukrainian church looks higher that it is in reality. This illusion was achieved by a gradual diminution of stories and rhythmic repetition of lines and decorations.

Inside the churches were furnished with representations that served as Bible for the illiterate. They served as treasure-houses, libraries, shrines and fortresses during wars.

Among the structures of princely Ukraine the St. Sophia Cathedral of Kyiv occupies a special place. It was built to mark the victory of the Kyivan Prince Yaroslav the Wise over the nomadic Pechenegs. The golden dome of he Cathedral can be seen from all the hills of present-day Kyiv. The Cathedral consists of five naves. The main volume of the structure is surrounded by two rows of galleries; their open arches connect the building with the environment. The whole complex is crowned with thirteen drums with a high central dome. The interior of the Cathedral is decorated with fresco paintings and mosaics; it is one of the best art ensembles of the early Middle Ages.

Among other monuments of the 11th–12th centuries the Cathedral of Our Savior in Chernihiv, the Dormition Cathedral of the Kyiv-Pechersk Lavra, the St. Michael's Monastery of the Golden Domes, and the remnants of the Golden Gate are of special value.

43
Rocky fortifications of Kamyanets-Podilsk

44
The Trinity Cathedral in Hustyn Monastery

45
Dormition Cathedral in Kyiv-Pechersk Lavra

46
St. Sophia Cathedral in Kyiv

VIP КАЗИНО ПРЕМЕР ПАЛАЦ

In the 14th–16th centuries the influence of western Gothic and Renaissance spread in Ukraine. Severe Gothic style found its reflection in the construction of fortresses and castles that came to substitute for old wooden fences.

The most powerful defensive work in Ukraine of that time were the Akermanska Fortress (present-day Bilhorod Dnistrovsky in Odesa Oblast), and the rocky fortifications of Kamianets-Podilsky in Khmelnytsky Oblast.

Among old castles, the former residences of princes and magnates, Verkhniy Zamok (Upper Castle) in Lutsk has been preserved best of all.

Resting upon antique samples Renaissance architecture came to Ukraine predominantly from Italy. Coordinating their creative concepts with the peculiarities of surrounding landscape and the requirements of local customers, Italian architects created the famous architectural ensemble *Rynok* in Lviv. Korniakt's palace built for the rich Greek merchant is the most imposing building in the square. An outstanding monument of the Renaissance is the

architectural ensemble of the *Lviv Brotherhood* — the Ukrainian Orthodox community of the city. The main structure of the ensemble is the *Dormition Church*. The 65-meter-high bell tower built on Korniakt's money and named after him and the Chapel of Three Hierarchs stand nearby.

The famous khan palace in Bakhchisaray built by Italian masters remains one of the most exotic architectural monuments of the 16th–18th centuries in the Crimea.

In the 17th–18th centuries, when Cossack Ukraine gained its own statehood after the bloody war of liberation, Ukrainian architec-

47
Present-day Kyiv

48
Odesa Archeology Gallery

49
Paton bridge in Kyiv at night

50
Griffins — adornments of old buildings

ture achieved flourishing years. Hetmans' ambitions were fully satisfied by baroque that reigned in Europe at that time. Under the influence of western tradition the style known as "Ukrainian baroque" came into being. Its exceptional splendor manifested itself in majestic temples symbolizing numerous victories of Cossack arms. The walls of the structures were decorated with vertical strips that created an impression of embroidered towels, or were fully covered with ornaments and symbolic designs. The generosity of Ukrainian land was embodied in garlands of flowers and leaves. Buildings constructed under Hetman Ivan Mazepa are particularly distinguished for their decorative magnificence.

In Hetmans' Ukraine churches became a subject of public concern and self-respect. Every urban and rural community considered it their honorable duty to build a church and the best one at that. As a result architectural masterpieces sprang up in the provinces exciting the envy of capital cities: the *Sorochyntsi Church* in Poltava province, founded by Hetman Danylo Apostol, the *Trinity Cathedral* of the Hustyn monastery in Chernihiv province, the *Transfiguration Cathedral* at the Mharsk monastery near Lubny in Poltava province, the *Intercession Cathedral* in Kharkiv.

The transition from luxuriant and splendid baroque to carefree rococo that took place in the late 17th – early 18th centuries is represented by the bell tower and the gate in the fence of St. Sophia Cathedral of Kyiv built by the German architect Johann Schädel. The highest achievement of the architect became the bell tower of the Kyiv-Pechersk Lavra. It is 96 meters high and has no analogues in Ukraine.

St. Andrew's Church in Kyiv built after the design of the court architect Bartolomeo Rastrelli was the first creation of pure rococo in Ukraine. By the lightness of its forms and proportions it looks like a park pavilion rather than a building for public worship. Rising on a high steep slope overlooking the Dnipro it seems to soar in the air.

The splendid decorative portals, pediments, gates and ornamented windows and doors of *Mariinsky Palace* in Kyiv deserve special attention. Ivan Hryhorovych-Barsky, a Ukrainian pupil of Johann Schädel, was one of the creators of this masterpiece.

West European baroque taste prevailed in stone structures of the Right Bank and Western Ukraine, though the most outstanding monuments, such as the *Pochaiv Lavra* in Volyn and the *Cathedral of St. Yura* in Lviv, are marked by national features.

The period of the Hetmanite State coincided in time with the flourishing of wooden cult construction. Wooden churches and bell towers built at that time cannot but fascinate you with their lyricism, picturesque forms and technical perfection. The common constructive element of the walls and ceilings of all wooden churches is the framework of a rectangular or octahedral form, though the diversity of volume and space

51
Interior of St. Volodymyr's Cathedral

52
Lviv Opera-House

53
Mariinsnky Palace in Kyiv

54
Bird's eye view of St. Michael Square in Kyiv

solutions is really impressive. In spite of their small dimensions the churches produce an impression of monumentality that is intensified by spacious and high interiors. A true masterpiece of wooden architecture is the *Cathedral of Trinity* in Novoselytsi (present-day Novomoskovsk) — the only church with 9 drums in Ukraine, built in 1773–1781 by the self-taught master Yakym Pohrebniak.

In the turn of the 19th century classicism that followed the laconic and impressive forms of antique Greece and Rome became a dominating trend in European art. The establishment of this style took place at a time when Ukraine lost the remains of Cossack autonomy. That is why classicism spread in Ukraine by the mediation of Russian culture. A good example of classic reconstruction became the new downtown section of Poltava, and the rich newly built ensemble of *Prymorsky Boulevard* in Odesa. From the semicircular square in the center of which stands the monument to Richelieu, *Potiomkin Staircase* (192 steps) descends to the sea; the boulevard was flanked by the palace of Count Vorontsov with a colonnade and the building of the stock exchange.

While spreading among the Ukrainian nobility the classic style manifested itself in magnificent palace-and-park ensembles. The dignitaries were followed by the landlords who built up thousands of "Greek-Roman" courtyards all over Ukraine: with porticoes, colonnades and triangle pediments on the facades.

The French variant of classic style in combination with Polish baroque and rococo spread widely in western Ukrainian lands. It was in this style that the *Ossolinsky Library* and *Skarbek Theatre* were built in Lviv.

55
A castle in Korsun-Shevchenkivsky

56
Khotyn castle

57
Rocky church in St. Clement monastery

58
Fortress ruins in Kamyanetsk-Podilsky

While passing by housing estates of Ukrainian towns you will see a change in artistic tastes that took place in the late 19th – early 20th centuries. Architectural structures in modernist style, declaring open subjectivism, were built at that period. The first attempt of a certain synthesis of arts in Ukrainian national spirit was made by brothers Vasyl and Fedir Krychevsky who initiated the construction of *Poltava Zemstvo* (elective district council). The program of national style was realized by Vasyl Krychevsky in the building of *People's Home* in Lokhvytsi, and the Memorial Museum near the grave of Taras Shevchenko in Kaniv. The Ukrainian national-democratic aesthetics had high hopes for the development of this style, but the works of the Krychevsky brothers remained its higher attainment.

Between World War I and II constructivism came to Ukrainian architecture for a short time, leaving its trace in the form of *Dzerzhinsky Square* in Kkarkiv (1925–1939); searches for the revival of old Ukrainian traditions found their reflection

in the building of *Ukrainian Agricultural Academy* in Kyiv (1925–1930).

Socialist epoch found its expression in architecture as well. An example of heavy "heroic" architecture is the *government building* of the Ukrainian SSR. To counterbalance it the building

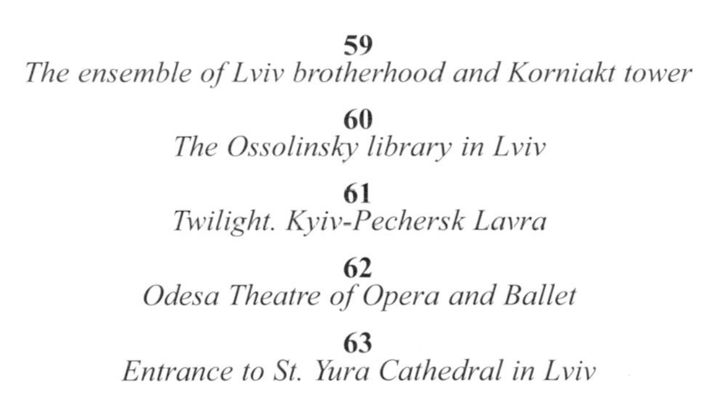

59
The ensemble of Lviv brotherhood and Korniakt tower

60
The Ossolinsky library in Lviv

61
Twilight. Kyiv-Pechersk Lavra

62
Odesa Theatre of Opera and Ballet

63
Entrance to St. Yura Cathedral in Lviv

ВОКЗАЛ
ПІВДЕННИЙ

of *Verkhovna Rada* of the Ukrainian SSR was built in 1936–1939 by the architect V. Zabolotny. The influence of imperial style — the so-called Stalinist neoclassicism — remained in the official structures of that period.

The post-war decade was not the time for architectural innovations: every effort was made to restore ruined cities and villages. Kyiv was built according to an overall plan. Competition announced for the best project of building up Khreschatyk Street resulted in the emergence of the architectural ensemble that remains the city's adornment even today. Among public structures erected by Ukrainian architects in the first half of the 1950s a special place is occupied by *Sailor's Club* in Sevastopol; in 1958 the *Exhibition of Advanced Methods in the National Economy* was completed in Kyiv. A top-priority task in the 1960s – 70s was the construction of dwelling houses. Architects and builders searched for optimal ways of resolving this problem. The *Palace of Culture "Ukraina"* and the building of the *Institute of Technical Information* were also built in those years.

At present buildings of heightened comfort are being erected at a rapid pace, and architectural monuments of the past, primarily churches, are being renovated.

64
Southern railway station in Kyiv

65
Building of Verkhovna Rada of Ukraine

66
A modern traffic intersection

67
Pysanka museum in Kolomyia

НЕСТОР - ЛІТОПИСЕЦЬ

LANGUAGE

Spoken by 45 million people in the world the Ukrainian language belongs to the Slavic group of Indo-European languages. The Ukrainian language, as well as Russian and Byelorussian, developed on the basis of the dialects of the old Rus language. The most important phonetic, grammatical and lexical peculiarities of the Ukrainian language were conceived in the time of Kyivan Rus. Old Slavic lexemes that have remained unchangeable number about 2,000, and the number of words built up on this basis and loan words is nearly 150,000. At the same time the Ukrainian vocabulary contains many words unknown to other Slavic languages.

The Ukrainians' ancestors became proficient in writing as long ago as the 6th–8th centuries. They had two alphabets: Glagolitic and Cyrillic ones. After the introduction of Christianity Cyrillic alphabet became firmly established.

The oldest examples of the Ukrainian language have come down to us in the form of numerous songs, ballads and Cossack chronicles.

The first grammar of the Ukrainian language was composed in 1643 ("Slavonic Grammar" by *Ivan Uzhevych*). The beginning of the new Ukrainian literary language was laid by the poet and playwright, the founder of the Ukrainian drama *Ivan Kotliarevsky*, and the basic role in its formation was played by *Taras Shevchenko*. The great Ukrainian poet did not confine himself to a certain dialect, but collected the most typical words and grammatical constructions from the folk language as a whole. Besides, he widely used the best features of the old Ukrainian language, enriching its vocabulary with necessary neologisms and foreign words.

It is to the credit of *Panteleimon Kulish*, a writer and political figure, that he worked out the Ukrainian alphabet. Used for the first time in 1856 and later reformed by *Borys Hrinchenko* in

68
Nestor the Chronicler

69–71
Pages from old chronicles

"Dictionary of the Ukrainian Language" (1908), this alphabet has underlined present-day Ukrainian phonetic orthography.

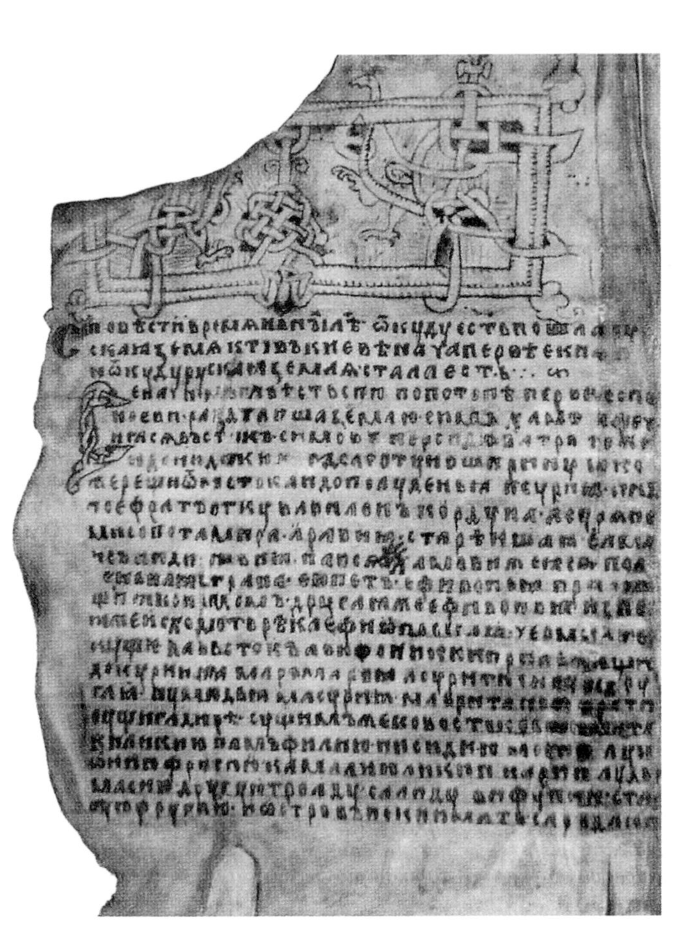

The Ukrainian alphabet consists of 33 letters. Besides, in writing it has two special signs: apostrophe and accent. The Ukrainian language is somewhat difficult for foreigners to study. Thus, Ukrainian words have three genders: masculine, feminine and neuter, they change by numbers and persons (verbs) or by numbers and cases (nouns). Understanding the language is complicated by mobile accent which, as a rule, change the meaning of the word. Word order is free. This, in contrast, facilitates the process of learning.

The Ukrainian language is rich in proverbs, sayings and riddles that represent memory of the people, conclusions from life experience; they demonstrate the people's views on ethics, morals, history and the policy of society.

The Ukrainian language is extraordinarily image-bearing and melodious. In spite of its beauty and richness it had for a long time to prove its right to existence, just as the Ukrainian people on the whole. There were periods when the Ukrainian language was partially or fully prohibited. According to Russian emperors' ukases the "little Russian dialect" was only allowed on the stage and in publications as a dialect reality, but not in serious scientific or literary texts, i.e. the language of high professional culture was prohibited. The essence of the emperors' prohibitions laid in their striving to turn Ukraine into part of the provinces. Ukrainian was officially acknowledged as a separate language after the revolution of 1905.

In independent Ukraine the Ukrainian language has been proclaimed the official language. It is the language of public and political institutions, the mass media, theater, science and engineering, each citizen of Ukraine can freely use it everyday life.

72
The classroom of the Ukrainian philosopher Hryhoriy Skovoroda in Pereyasliv collegium

73
An old manuscript

74
The first page of A Tale of Bygone Centuries — the oldest chronicle of the Eastern Slavs

75
A miniature from the Ostromyrov Gospel

OLD BELIEFS

Faith belongs to the fundamental bases of a human being, it emerged together with man and helps him become himself. Our predecessors did not differ from the world surrounding them, they just looked for their place in it, and with that which stood against them or was alien to them they tried to come to an agreement, to include in their own space, to settle their interrelations through sacrifice, rituals, rites, and word. Thus four elements (fire, air, water, earth) were the objects of worship of our predecessors, the old Slavs; heavenly bodies — sun, stars and moon; plants and trees, beasts and birds. Ukrainian folklore and the ritual-custom culture have brought to our days the remains of that old world outlook. Among them are bewitching insects and wild animals, moon, rain, thunder rituals. Christian chroniclers ironically noted that the heathens believed in sneezing and croaking. Really, numerous medieval manuscript collections of useful pieces of advice describing magic and mystic actions, various miracles, the so-called Thunder books, and Lightning books were copied and circulated among the people until the early 20th century. Until recently the residents of Zhytomyr Oblast greeted sunrise with the words: "God be praised! It is already light!" They said it rejoicing over the fact that the sun was in the sky, that a new day came, and that life continued. Pediments of Polissia houses in Volyn are decorated with small suns even today; it is believed they protect against any evil. In former times, with the same purpose sun was carved on the tie beams of traditional Ukrainian houses, sometimes moon and stars, and later cross, were placed beside. In winter nature sleeps, the sun does not warm, and shines stingily at that, so it was good to come to understanding with storm and blizzard so that they wouldn't harm in the future. For this purpose at Christmas frost and storm were invited "to eat boiled rice," hoping that being gratified in that way they would not appear in spring and in summer.

There is mention in chronicles about the worship of springs and streams. Land without water turns into a desert, so that is why even today every well in Ukraine is taken care of, and provided with a curb or sweep.

According to popular belief birds that returned from the south brought on their wings warmth and spring to the native land. In Polissia it is a custom to greet storks, cranes and wild-geese by throwing up a wisp of straw or hay saying: "That's for your nests, and for warm summer." In folk poetry man is often compared to a plant or a tree: a girl is as beautiful as a flower, and as slender as a poplar; a Cossack is as strong as an oak tree; a child is growing like a pussy-willow. An idea of the World tree the roots of which are underground and the crown is in the sky is known, as an original model of the world, not only to the Slavs, but to other peoples as well. Here all makes up a single whole — the dead who left for the lower world, living people from the middle visible world, and gods from the heavenly heights. The representation of the World tree that was also perceived as the family-tree is widespread in folk embroidery and home decoration. In imagination of our forefathers the world was inhabited, apart from them, by various invisible spirits. Forest nymphs and wood goblins lived in the forests, water-sprites and red and white mermaids in water, and house-spirits in houses. The unwritten code of customs regulated relations with representatives of this mysterious invisible world; keeping to them it was possible to avoid undesirable contacts. Thus, for instance, felling "the main tree" in the forest was prohibited, just as throwing garbage into the water, walking into the field on Whitsunday, putting matches on the table, etc.

Our predecessors' poetic concept of nature, that has been preserved in folk poetry and custom culture, testifies to certain ecological cleanness of folk culture the main law of which was personal responsibility for bad deeds which, according to popular world outlook, could result in elemental adversity. Glorifying nature, the creation of God, people accordingly extolled the Creator himself, thanking Him for rain and the sun, for the beauty of the young moon, and for a new day that has come.

76
The Zbruchansk stone image with the representations of the pagan deities Mokosh, Veles, Perun and Lada

77
A pagan alter

FOLK HOLIDAYS AND RITES

Folk customs, traditions and rites are invisibly linked with ethnos in space and time, preventing them from disappearance in other peoples and cultures. Calendar rites are one of the oldest layers of Ukrainian folk culture. Called to life by practical needs of the plowman, they reflected special conditions of nature on the days of solstices, and seasonal fluctuations. The power of the word, music, dances and ritual acts were called forth to render harmless evil, to give man good health, a bumper crop and well-being. After adopting Christianity these holidays entered into the church calendar, although with considerable changes.

Formerly new year in Ukraine was marked in spring and coincided in time with the beginning of field work. A new agricultural year started on *Candlemas Day* (Feb.2, O.S.). According to popular belief Winter meets with Spring on that day and they start fighting each trying to get the upper hand. A thaw on that day promised near spring and a good pasture.

Birds were the harbingers of spring. They were waited for from the holiday Invention of the Head of John the Baptist (Feb.24 O. S.) that in popular etymology became the holiday of birds' return from the south.

Pancake week was celebrated late in February — early March. Man of straw symbolizing winter was burned in the fire. Pancakes looking like the sun were fried everywhere. Young people amused themselves with music, and tying up special ribbons to the arms of those who failed to marry in the current year; the latter paid off by wetting a bargain.

There was a popular belief that on Lady Day, the very same day when the angel Gabriel brought his announcement to Mary, God annually blessed the earth, plants and "all kinds of breathing." According to Hutsul belief he put his head in the earth to warm it, that everything alive in the earth wake up. Work on the land before the holiday was prohibited.

Adoption of Christianity made our ancestors to believe that they are immortal due to the Resurrection. Formerly Easter was just the holiday of spring resurrection of nature. It was preceded by Lent, a period of spiritual and bodily purification. On the last Sunday before Lent it was customary to ask one's relatives' and neighbors' pardon.

On Palm Sunday pussy-willow was consecrated in the church and people wished one another good health and wealth. The consecrated twig of pussy-willow was used to turn cow out to grass for the first time, and to bake brown paskha. On the eve of Easter people baked Easter cakes and painted Easter eggs. According to popular belief on this holiday the sun is shining brightly, water in rivers and wells becomes curative when the bells start ringing, announcing the Resurrection of Christ. The whole world seemed to unite in the joy of spring awakening. Relatives visited each other, godfathers brought presents to their god-children, children went to see their relatives and neighbors and greet them with the holiday.

The pagan holiday of luxuriant greenery — Green Sunday — became Whitsunday and is marked on the day of The Descent of the Holy Spirit. The day before houses were decorated with maple and birch twigs, a sow thistle was placed on the gate as protection against evil forces. On Whitsunday mermaids go out from the water and stroll about the field the whole week and dance in rye, improving its growth.

78
Shrovetide — a farewell to winter

79
A girl in spring

80
The clearing power of the midsummer night fire

St. John the Baptist's day (Midsummer Night, 24 June O. S.) was the day of summer solstice, which meant that the sun already turns to winter, and nature begins to go out. That is probably why this holiday was particularly merry and rakish. Young people jumped across a fire to have a pair, swam and had a shower-bath, girls sang songs, danced, and told fortunes by wreaths throwing them into the water. "John's herbs" gathered in the morning — St. John's wort, camomile, origanum, willow herb — were considered particularly healing. Those who wanted to become rich or proficient in some secret knowledge searched for fern flower.

Cheese cakes were cooked for the holiday of St. Peter (1 Jul. O.S.), and shepherds were offered a treat. It was the beginning of harvest season and to make it a success farmers mowed the first sheaf for "Peter's cap."

The cycle of autumn holidays began with the Transfiguration when the harvest of earthly fruit was gathered, and when God was exalted for his generous gifts. On the Intercession (Oct. 1 O.S.) the ground was already covered with leaves or snow. Unmarried women and young girls addressed the Virgin Mary with a request for husband. Those who built houses were in a hurry to enter their new homes on the holiday so as to be always under the intercession of the Mother of God.

Winter holidays opened a new year of human life. At Christmas (Dec. 25 O.S.) Christ was born giving people a possibility to live in love, peace and accord. The cycle of Ukrainian winter holidays, from Christmas to Epiphany, was directed exactly at the creation of such a new and harmonious world. Boiled rice, wheat, etc. with raisins and honey (kutia), and twelve meager dishes are cooked for Christmas. According to tradition enemies were to make it up with each other in order to live in peace and harmony in the new year. Midwives delivered supper to god-fathers and god-mothers, grandmothers and grandfathers. Young people and children went Christmas caroling to cheer up and amuse the villagers. There could be several groups of carol-singers. with Bethlehem star or with puppet-show that, according to the scenario, had three Magi, king Herod, as well as a Gypsy, Soldier, an Old Man and Woman. Part of the raised money was transferred to the church.

Figured cakes — "young lady" and "gee-gee" — were baked or bought for children. Kutia was boiled for New Year and Epiphany as well, people paid visits to one another, greeting with holidays. Well-wishers went from home to home symbolically scattering grains of wheat on the floor for a good harvest next year, and wishing well-being to the master and mistress of the house. Sometimes they were invited to share a meal. On Epiphany water was consecrated in the church and in wells. Farmers who had bee-gardens treated people to honey near a well so that they had more honey in the future. Water was used to consecrate the household, and it was kept just in case of "the evil eye" and illness.

Winter comes to an end. The sun born at Christmas becomes warmer and warmer, reviving the land in spring so that the grain thrown into the earth would grow into good harvest, and that life would last always.

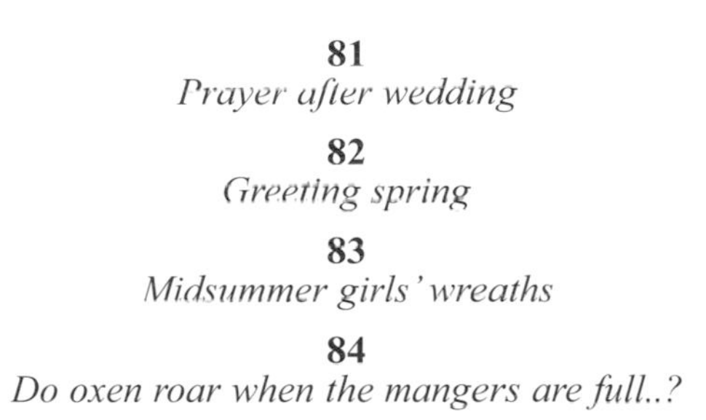

81
Prayer after wedding

82
Greeting spring

83
Midsummer girls' wreaths

84
Do oxen roar when the mangers are full..?

FOLK CULTURE

Generous giftedness of the Ukrainian people has always attracted attention of researchers who noted its well-developed feeling of the beautiful. This was promoted by beautiful natural environment and the mode of life full of rituals and rites closely connected with nature and seasons of the year. Family and public rites resembled original plays in several acts. Children acquired the models of world arrangement and conduct from childhood. The most important duty of parents was to teach their children "customs." Not to do this was considered a great sin.

Verbal formulas and ritual acts were handed down from generation to generation. Events from the life of nature left an imprint on the consciousness, giving birth to rich creative expression. An eternal bent for the beautiful showed itself in everyday life. As Christianity spread the initial natural core was supplemented by another one — church.

The powerful cultural structure was shaken by the cataclysms of the 20th century: three revolutions, two wars, famines organized by the communist regime, Stalin's repressions.

Traditional Ukrainian settlements can only be seen today at *museums of folk architecture and life* in the open which are located in Kyiv, Lviv, Uzhgorod, Pereyaslav-Khmelnytsky and Chernivtsi.

Formerly Ukrainian settlements were placed in river valleys and gullies protected from the wind. The famous Ukrainian peasant's mud and straw white huts were scattered in the shadow of luxuriant trees and bushes. A hut for a Ukrainian was not just a living space. It personified the world outlook of the people. The ceiling and roof reflected the heavenly spiritual world; the walls, windows and doors symbolized earthly life and human intercourse; the floor and threshold were perceived as the border between the earthly and underground kingdoms. The hut was ornamented both outside and inside: it was whitewashed, outlined at the bottom, and painted with flower ornaments. It was esthetic and had a magic meaning: the exclusive circle protected the family from evil spirits and various misfortunes.

Laying the foundation of a new dwelling, its building and giving a house-warming party were special ceremonies. Family hearth — the stove — was a sacral place in the hut. It was treated like a living being that presented the family with heat, calm and well-being. Home icon was placed in the corner with face towards the east. The table was placed under the icon and was meant for honorable guests and newly weds. The hut looked at the world with its own "eyes" — windows. Window-panes were made of ox-bladders, then of mica, and later of glass. The threshold was a symbol of the beginning and the end of the hut. Those going to the alter or on the last journey paid homage to the threshold. A horseshoe was nailed on the threshold or above the door. According to popular belief it brought happiness to the family. To speak or to hand something across the threshold was considered a bad sign.

85
Near the well

86
A village church

87
A traditional Ukrainian hut

88
Pokuttia — a corner in a room adorned with icons

Special consideration was given to the building and decoration of cult structures — churches and bell-towers. Folk church architecture had its own peculiarities in each region of Ukraine. But in each case the church dominated the surroundings.

History has not preserved many names of self-taught masters whose creations enrapture today the whole world. One of them, Yakym Pohrebniak, is the author of the only nine-drum church in Ukrainian wooden architecture which is to be found in Novoselytsi (present-day Novomoskovsk, Dnipropetrovsk Oblast).

According to a folk tale Yakym boasted at a Cossack council that he would build a nine-drum church by himself. But after the foundation of the church was laid the builder disappeared no one knew where. He returned in a few days, exhausted but happy, with a model of the church plaited of rods. It turned out that Yakym had been frightened by the scale of his intention and run away from the village. He went over in his mind again and again all the stages of building, but as soon as he reached the top his calculations proved mistaken and the structure tumbled down. Because of overstrain he fell into slumber. In his sleep he saw St. Nicholas the Miracle-Worker who told him how

to build the church. On waking up the master made the model after which he created his masterpiece.

All architectural structures and home utensils were decorated predominantly with carved geometric ornaments. Carved iconostases were particularly distinguished for their extraordinarily decorative wealth. Their ornamental motifs — vine, sun flowers, hollyhocks and roses — created a surprising embroidered work. A great many of these outstanding works of folk wood-carving were annihilated together with the churches.

89
St. Michael's Church in Pyrohovo

90
Before the altar

91–92
Ukrainian painted Easter eggs

93
Earthenware toys

Ukrainian ornaments have preserved some elements of primeval symbolism and the images of old gods. Ukraine was the motherland of the architectural ornament meander. Things decorated with such a design were found in excavations of the settlements of the Stone Age in Mizyn and Chernihiv regions. The rectilinear ornament symbolized continuity and endlessness; the diamond-shaped pattern — fertility; swastika — fire; zoomorphic images — totem animals and birds.

Ornaments decorate world-famous Ukrainian *pysanka* (painted Easter eggs). Triangles, spirals, circles etc. were the signs of different rituals linked with the cult of the Sun or sacred numbers.

Ornament became the most wide-spread in embroidery and carpet-weaving. The famous Ukrainian embroidered shirts, towels and carpets remain to be an inexhaustible shrine of folk fantasy. A stylized female figure with raised hands was an embodiment of the protectress of life. A wavy branch with stylized ducks, peacocks, roosters, and doves symbolized the Tree of Life. The motif *Barvinok* (Periwinkle) is the symbol of unfading life. The design *Apple Circle* symbolizes love.

Symbolic meaning of *rushnyks* (embroidered towels) is to bless and guard, to hold the nearest and dearest in remembrance. Rushnyks were hung at places of honor and worthy of note: over icons, family portraits, doors and windows. By tradition the bread and salt of welcome were placed on *rushnyk*, it was a must when entering new home, swaddling baby and greeting newly-weds. Rushnyks are used when lowering the coffin into the grave, to tie up the arms of the cross, to cover the tombstone on funeral repast.

Artistic tableware was made for dishes and drinks. Bowls, spoons, mugs and ladles were made of strong and patterned wood species: birch, linden, pear-tree. The handicrafts were planed, ground, poli-

94
Braiding straw

95
Potters

96
Wood engraving articles

97
A spinning-wheel

shed and then painted with stylized patterns of golden and dark-red colors. Ceramic ware made on potter's wheel was distinguished for its refined forms and decoration: pots, bowls, small barrels and jugs in the form of a wheel. In old times there were many pottery centers in Ukraine but only a few have survived to this day. Traditional ceramics (tableware, decorative sculpture, children's toys) are only produced in Opyshnia and Poltava region.

The production of glass was known in Ukraine as long ago as princely times. Quartz sand, chalk, lime, different kinds of refractory clay, charcoal, resin and potash were used as raw materials. Bottles, flasks, goblets, wine-glasses, vases were adorned with intricate ornaments and covered with enamels or gold. The traditions of artistic glassware production have been preserved in Ukraine up to the present.

Ironware of blacksmiths and smelters was artistically decorated as well: details for carts, gates, doors, bells. Goldsmiths and silversmiths produced earrings, finger-rings, wedding rings, icon settings. Lately the art of goldsmithery has begun to revive.

Due to highly developed weaving the Ukrainians had good taste and knew how to dress well. Various kinds of cloth were made at home, raw materials for weaving being flax, hemp, wool, and later cotton and paper yarn. Leather and plaited clothes were also used in everyday life. The wealthy could afford cloths of foreign make: silk, taffeta, brocade, velvet. Cloths were dyed different colors using natural dyes. Each color had a symbolic meaning: white implied

98
The hazel eyes and the black brows...

99
Embroidered patterns

100
With a smile to the future

101
Zhytomyr beading school

102
Match-makers are coming

hope; yellow — sun, fire, ripe crops in the field; blue — the sky and the air; green — spring and revival; red — living blood; black — a dark night.

All kinds of clothes were adorned with embroidery, fine needlework being an occupation exclusively for women. They used for this every appropriate occasion: long autumn and winter evenings, hours of rest. More than a hundred embroidery techniques are known in Ukraine. One of the most perfect is embroidery in white with latticework. Popular enough is cross-stitch embroidery. A great colorist effect is produced by the combination of red and black. Multi-colored embroideries are impressive for their color concord and contrast and tender transition of one color into another. Reshetylivka in Poltava Oblast is a well-known center of embroidery.

From childhood every Ukrainian girl stocked up with embroideries. A good girl was considered the one who could "sew and embroider, and sing songs." Dressed in embroidered clothing a Ukrainian woman looked like a bouquet of natural flowers.

Women's and men's underwear were a linen night-gown and a night-shirt respectively. They were adorned with embroidered patterns on the chest, the ends of the sleeves and the neck. These patterns protected their owners against danger, hence the saying "to be born in a shirt" which means to be born with a silver spoon in one's mouth.

Over night-gowns women put on woolen *zapaska* (a skirt of to pieces) and *plakhta* (a wraparound skirt). *Zapaska* was made of two narrow flaps — the front one and the back one. Night-gown peeped out on each side and at the front. *Plakhta* consisted of one piece of fabric. It was wrapped around the waist and hips making the woman's figure particularly attractive.

Men wore linen or woolen pants usually of white color and narrow at the foot. Sharovary (loose trousers) were worn on holidays, were made of red or blue cloth and were "as wide as the Black Sea." They were an indispensable piece of Cossack clothing.

Of outer clothing *kozhukh* (sheepskin coat) was the most widespread. The technology of its production was rather labor-consuming. The number and quality of *kozhykhs* testified to the prosperity of the family. When a baby was born he/she was placed on the *kozhukh* fur in order "happiness does not shun the babe." During a wedding newly-weds had also to sit on *kozhukh* "in order to be rich." *Kozhukh* was worn mainly in winter. In summer man was protected against bad weather by svyta — a home-woven garment made of cloth.

Head-dress was a matter of principle for women. At any season of the year women were to wear a head kerchief. Embroidered kerchiefs were presented as the guard to those leaving for war. Kerchiefs were used to wrap in bread for the journey, they were tied to the arms of participants in rites. Married women wore *ochipky* — little caps with special signs or kerchiefs tied to them.

Women had no right under any circumstances "to show their hair." The well-known ethnographer F. Vovk (1847–1918) noted that Ukrainian women could bare their legs without any ceremony, but

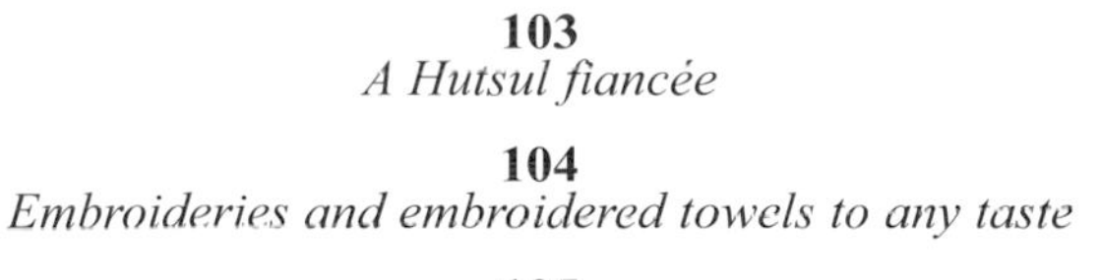

103
A Hutsul fiancée

104
Embroideries and embroidered towels to any taste

105
Old Ukrainian clothing

106
Blacksmith

would never agree to uncover their heads. Only girls were allowed to put up their hair "for show." On holidays and festivals girls braided their hair in two plaits round the head, adorning them with colour fillets or wreaths of natural flowers.

Weather being warm men covered their heads with straw hats, and when it was freezing they put on fur-caps made of lamb skins. To go out in the street without a cap was a bad sign. In contrast, when entering a home or sitting at the table it was to be taken off by all means. The same was to be done when meeting the elders or guests.

Out of clothing accessories belts were made with special inspiration. Apart from their practical function they served as protection against evil force. Men's belts were wide (up to 30 cm) and long (up to 3 m). Women's belts were as long and wide. They were woven or braided of wool, flax or hemp, and died black, blue or green, and adorned with whimsical ornament. *Cheresy* — leather belts to which small purses, various vessels and metal hatchets were fixed were widespread in the mountain regions of the Carpathians.

Ukrainian women are notable for their special love for adornments. Even the poorest had their own necklace — a chest adornment

of coral, amber. garnets, glass or smalt. Necklace was worn always. It was considered to have magic properties. *Dukaty* and *dukachi* were another protecting adornment. It was a string of silver coins and jewelry worn as a necklace. After the introduction of Christianity crosses were included as well. At the age of two Ukrainian girls had their ears pierced for earrings. Jewelry was handed down from generation to generation as a family relic.

The Ukrainians have won the fame of an extraordinarily musical people. Ukrainian choirs have no equals in the world. Ukrainian church singing is also one of the best in the world. Most of the Ukrainian

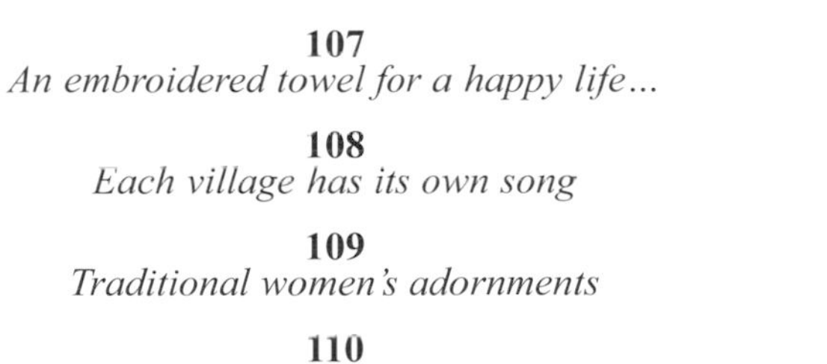

107
An embroidered towel for a happy life...

108
Each village has its own song

109
Traditional women's adornments

110
Bee-garden attached to Kyiv-Pechersk Lavra

singers have no special education but have an inherent good ear for music.

A capella, singing without instrumental accompaniment, is particularly popular.

Kobza and *bandura* are the main folk musical instruments. They have long bass strings drawn along the neck and short strings over the sounding board. *Trembita* is a wide-spread instrument in Western Ukraine. It is a long wooden pipe (up to 2.5 m) broadened at the end, made of a piece of wood and wrapped up in birch bark. Trembita utters a sorrowful and strong sound that can be heard at a distance of 10 kilometers.

Bubon (a kind of tambourine) is a wide hoop covered with a close-fitting skin. Small metal plates are put into the openings, and a piece of wire with jingle bells is drawn crosswise inside. They play *bubon* with one hand, beating time with palm and fingers. *Bubon* together with a fiddle and *basola* (a variety of cello) make up a trio — "*troista muzyka*" — that plays on high days and holidays.

In olden times every natural phenomenon and production process was accompanied with choir and musical ceremonies, and calendar and wedding songs.

Bylina was composed in princely times, and in Cossack times *duma* came into being — a lyrical and epic work on the struggle of the Ukrainian people against the Tatars, Turks, Poles and other conquerors of Ukraine. Paradoxically as it may seem the *dumas* do not contain any battle or bloody scenes. The sorrowful motifs render the feeling of regret about devastation, and glorify recalcitrance, fortitude and a call for freedom and happiness.

Kobza-players passed *dumas* on from one generation to another. Blinded by the enemy the minstrels accompanied the Cossack army, spreading their glory all over Ukraine. *Dumas* were not sung. They were performed as recitative accompanied by *kobza* or *bandura*. Each performer composed a melody of his own.

The song has been upholding the Ukrainian national self-consciousness till now. Song festivals are held today in different regions of the country.

Due to the picture *Cossack Mamay* Ukrainian folk painting became famous all over the world. Starting in the 18th century it was painted on the walls and doors of the huts, on little chests, plates and linen.

The picture portrays a Cossack sitting with a kobza in his hands against a landscape. His true comrade, horse, is standing nearby. Inscription written in verse tells about Cossack feats of arms.

Ukrainian fairs remain the favorite places of festive spare time. Annually in August the famous Soroshinsky Fair takes place in the homeland of the great writer-mystifier of the 19th century Nilolai Gogol. Like a hundred years ago sellers and purchasers come here from everywhere. Here you can buy an amusing wild beast, and a live pig, a straw bread-basket and a modern combine. Besides, the present-day Sorochintsi Fair is a peculiar museum and theater in the open. The incomparable color of Gogol's remote times is recreated by the clean whitewashed huts under thatched roofs, idyllic windmills, cane-covered granaries. Dramatized performances and folklore groups appear on the stage against this background.

111
An old kobza-player

112
The Cossack Mamay

113
Bagpipes...

корчма

TRADITIONAL CUISINE

The saying goes that the one who eats well, works well. Traditional Ukrainian dishes that have remained popular up today number 70 names.

Bread is the main daily food product in Ukraine. A loaf of bread was a must when stepping over the threshold of a new home, when meeting guests and seeing off newly-weds to the wedding. It was considered a sin not to eat up a slice of bread or to throw it onto the ground. Bread was baked mostly of rye; white bread was baked on solemn occasions. Daily bread is called *palianytsia*. It was baked of leavened dough in a thoroughly heated stove, the loaves being placed on cabbage leaves. It remained fresh and flavored for several weeks. The traditional method of bread baking has been preserved in some villages up to this day. Ceremonial bread — *korovay* (round loaf) — can always be seen at Ukrainian weddings. It is much more in size than *palianytsia*, baked of the best kinds of flour. On top it is ornamented with symbolic patterns made also of dough. Sweet *paskha* (Easter cake), another kind of ceremonial bread, is baked once a year, at Eastertide.

Varenyky is a usual dish for each Ukrainian family. It has been known in Ukraine since the 16th century. Real *varenyky* are made of insipid boiled dough stuffed with meat, cabbage, cheese, haricot, cherry, apple, plum, poppy-seed or guelder rose. If you add some sour cream or honey to cheese, fruit or berry *varenyky*, you will get the most delicious food. The saying "to bathe like a varenyk in sour cream" is well known to each Ukrainian and means to have a prosperous and carefree life.

Another favorite dish of the Ukrainians is *halushky* (a kind of dumplings) — small balls or pellets of dough boiled in water or soup. They are enriched with fried onion and pork fat and eaten together with the broth. For unknown reasons *halushky* are associated with the Poltava region. Perhaps it is due to the fact that during the Russian-Swedish war of the early 18th century Poltava women fed the whole army of Peter I with *halushky* within a few hours.

Potato came to Ukraine in the second half of the 18th century and was called "another bread." Potatoes can be consumed as baked in their jackets, fried, boiled, as a separate dish or together with others.

It is generally known that the Ukrainians have a special liking for *pork fat*. It is usually eaten with bread or added to other dishes. It is an obligatory component of the so-called Cossack gruel, traditionally made of millet. A sufficient amount of pork fat on the table was a sign of real prosperity. A saying goes: "If I had been a landlord I'd have eaten pork fat and chased it with pork fat."

However, *borsch* was and remains to be the symbol of Ukrainian cuisine. Cooking borsch requires an extraordinary skill and a great many products (nearly 20). This dish has many varieties. The most popular one is *red borsch* made of cabbage, carrots,

114
The one who eats well, works well...

115–117
Dishes for the holiday:
boiled wheat with honey and ground poppy seeds for Christmas Eve, varenyky for New Year, and paskha for Easter

О'Панас

parsley, potatoes, onion and fermented with red beet or beet kvass. On high days and holidays *borsch* was boiled in broth with pork or chicken, on week-days it was enriched with pork fat pounded with garlic and onion. Some sour cream was added for taste. If you want to have a real taste of *borsch* you should eat it with a garlic *pampushka* (sort of bun), not with brown bread.

The main beverage after water was bread kvass. Out of spirits various kinds of *horilka* (vodka), *nastoyka*, fruit liqueur and beer remain the most popular.

Traditionally a Ukrainian family had four meals a day. Breakfast consisted of *kasha* (gruel), potatoes or pies; lunch — *borsch*, *kasha*, roast, nuts, fruit; snack before supper — pork fat, milk, sour cream, cheese; supper — soup, *halushky*, *varenyky*. Under the influence of Christianity it was considered a sin to consume meat, fat and eggs during the fasts and on the so-called "Lenten days" (Wednesday and Friday). The Ukrainians never consumed raw meat or fish.

The consumption of food was a peculiar ritual. Before laying the table the housewife covered it with a table-cloth and put tableware on the table. The whole family gathered at the table: the master of the house, his wife, their parents, sons, daughters, daughters-in-law, young children. Each one had his/her own place. After a thanksgiving prayer they proceeded to a meal. They ate with wooden spoons from a big common bowl. The meal proceeded steadily, without talk. Children who broke silence got a blow from their father with a spoon at their forehead. If during a meal a neighbor or a casual guest happened to come he was invited to the table.

Folk etiquette prohibited the guest eating much or grudgingly. After eating a few spoonfuls you were to wait for another offer. After meal they spoke and sang songs.

Naturally, times have changed and cuisine has changed as well. But Ukrainian dishes are traditionally cooked in each Ukrainian family even today and offered in restaurants and cafes.

118
You are welcome to restaurant Panas

119–121
Traditional dishes:
borsch, varenyky stuffed with cottage cheese and sour cream, stuffed potato

PROFESSIONAL CULTURE

Theatre

Ukrainian theatre was born in the depths of folk creative work and absorbed the peculiar romanticism of Ukrainian disposition. It has traversed a complicated path of evolution from the theatre of baroque epoch to the formation of the professional theatre of the late 19th century, the time of rapid development of dramatic art. The creative work of the directors Yosyp Stadnyk, Mykola Sadovsky and Les Kurbas played an important role in its establishment.

Present-day theatrical life in Ukraine is rather diversified. It embraces various directions and genres: from classic comedy to tragedy, from the avant-garde tendencies of the early 21th century, and the absurdity theatre to the post-modernist drama of today.

The repertoire of the drama theatres of Kyiv, Lviv, Odesa, Dnipropetrovsk and other cities includes works by foreign playrights and novelists (Edward Aldee, Thomas Mann, Samuel Becket, Anton Chekhov, Aleksandr Ostrovsky, Vladimir Nabokov, Jaroslav Haˇsek, James Joyce, Luigi Pirandello, Eugene Ionesci and others), as well as by Ukrainian authors (Ivan Franko, Vasyl Stefanyk, Lesia Ukrainka, Hryhoriy Skovoroda, Vasyl Stus, Lina Kostenko). The Ukrainian experimental theatre of today is characterized by its bent for the Far-Eastern reminiscences, which is revealed in its sensitivity to metaphysics, meditation, getting deeper into "the superior" and mystery, in combination with European stylistic models.

Lovers of recherché performance and perfect actor's mastery take pleasure in visiting the plays of "the theatre of one actor" of the creative amalgamation *Theatre in the Basket* in Lviv. Monoplays of the Kyiv theatre Actor produce an indelible impression. The Lviv spiritual theatre *Resurrection* concentrates on upholding the sacral function of dramatic art. It is putting on plays after the works of Pedro Calderon, George Byron, August Strindberg and others that urge the spectators to think about the mutual relation between the spiritual and artistic on the stage.

Ukrainian theatrical companies take an active part in Ukrainian and international festivals of dramatic art.

Cinema

The first attempts to create Ukrainian cinematograph were made back in the early 20th century. But it became famous only in the 1920s–30s due to the creative work of the film director Oleksandr Dovzhenko.

In the 1960s–70s Ukrainian cinema attained a success on the international scene (the film *The Shadows of Forgotten Ancestors* by the outstanding director Sergey Paradzhanov received 15 fes-

122
A scene from a play of Dnipropetrovsk Theatre of Opera and Ballet

123
Monument to Oleksandr Dovzhenko in his native land

tival awards, and his film *White Bird with a Black Sign* was awarded First Prize. Paradzhanov's films initiated Ukrainian "poetic cinema."

The Kyiv school of popular science film was known far and wide at that time as well.

There were six State film studios in Ukraine in the late 1980s. The most popular of them being the Oleksadr Dovzhenko Film Studio of Kyiv, and Odesa Film Studio.

In the late 1980s-early 90s cinema production in Ukraine was intensified, private initiative came into being, new studios were founded, and the number of films increased. Ukraine began to comprehend itself as a subject of history, and acquired its own cinematograph which was impossible in Soviet times.

The Ukrainian documentary film director Oleksandr Balahura was awarded First Prize at the international documentary festival in Florence for his film *To Our Sisters and Brothers* (1990). In 1992–1993 Oleksandr Rodniansky, director and general

producer of the TV company "Studio 1+1," made a valuable contribution to the development of the national documentary cinema. His films *Mission of Raul Wallenberg, Farewell to the USSR* and some others received numerous awards at the international film festivals in Munich, Valencia, Krakow, Polotsk, Yekaterinburg, Strasbourg, Leipzig and other cities. The last celebrated victory of the Ukrainian documentary cinema was the Golden Olive-Branch the young Kyiv director Ihor Strembytsky won for his short film Travelers at the 58th International Festival in Cannes.

124–125
Shooting the film The Gadfly, (director M. Maschenko)

The films *Melancholy Waltz* and *For the Home Hearth* by Borys Savchenko, and *The Notes of Snub-Nosed Mephistopheles* by Yuriy Liashenko were a discovery of the Ukrainian reality of the early 20th century. The screen presented the Ukrainian intelligentsia with their spiritual scarches and doubts, the eternal questions that have no answers.

Kira Muratova is probably the most fruitful Ukrainian film director of the late 20th–early 21st century. Her films are an endless gallery of marvelous and chimerical personages who oppose their environment and create it at the same time. Kira Muratova was awarded the prize of the American Fund of Independent Cinema for her film *A Letter to America* (1999) at the jubilee Berlinare — 50 (2000).

Film festivals *Molodist* (Youth) and *Vidkryta Nich* (The Open Night) have become known in the world and provide the latest novelties of Ukrainian cinema.

The national animation is developing quite successfully. The joint Ukraine-Russia festival *Krok* (Step) presents the latest cartoons.

Music

In the course of its centuries-old history the Ukrainian people created diversified musical folklore. Professional music has developed on the basis of folk musical culture. The creative work of Semion Hulak-Artemovsky, Mykola Lysenko, Kostiantyn Dankevych, Reingold Gliere, Anatoliy Kos-Anatolsky and other composers played an important role in the development of Ukrainian national music. The repertoire of the National Philharmonic Society in Kyiv and many concert halls all over Ukraine includes works by the classics of the national and world music, as well as by contemporary Ukrainian composers.

As of today Taras Shevchenko National Academic Theater of Opera and Ballet is the best opera and ballet company. Its opera and ballet groups performed on the stages of many foreign theatres, including the famous La Scala (Italy) and Metropolitan Opera (USA). It gave birth to the International ballet contest named after Serge Lifar who had been born and studied in Kyiv, the International festivals *Serge Lifar de la dance, Children and Stars of World Ballet*, and *Ave Verdi* devoted to the great Italian composer. The National Opera-House of Ukraine, Odesa Opera and Ballet Theatre and Lviv Opera-House are among the hundred of the best theatres of the world.

Choir singing is perhaps the most powerful field of the Ukrainian professional musical culture. The *Dumka* National Honored Academic Choir of Ukraine, Hryhoriy Veriovka State Ukrainian People's Choir, Kyiv Conservatoire Choir, V. Ikonnikov Chamber Choir and the Honored Ukrainian Choir of Bandura-players are well known throughout the world.

There are many variety groups in Ukraine that embrace different styles and answer different tastes: from hard rock, punk-rock, hip-hop to whimsical musical conglomerations with the elements of folk music. VV, Elza Ocean, Mandry and some other groups practice religious music. In 2004 the Ukrainian singer Ruslana came out winner of the Eurovision song contest which proved that Ukrainian pop-music is in keeping with world standards.

126
Ruslana, the winner of the Eurovision-2004 contest

127
A chamber choir performing

ΙC ΧC

Visual Arts

Icon-painting began to develop in Ukraine-Rus in the 10th century, after Prince Volodymyr baptized Kyivan Rus. Byzantine traditions were a model for local masters. Quite independent and original schools of icon-painting came into being later. Kyiv school was the most refined among them. Unfortunately, most of the works of the early Middle Ages have been lost. Chronicles alone have preserved records of the marvelous works by outstanding icon-painters, in particular Alipiy, a monk of the Kyiv-Pechersk Monastery.

Mosaics and frescos of St. Sophia Cathedral in Kyiv are the most distinguished among the memorials of monumental painting. Built during the reign of Prince Yaroslav the Wise this cathedral became one of the first monuments of old-Rus architecture.

After the Mongol-Tatar invasion and the decline of the Old-Rus State the Halychyna-Volyn principality inherited art traditions of

Kyivan Rus. The icon The *Virgin of Volyn*, a masterpiece of that time, originates exactly from Volyn.

The next flight of Ukrainian art falls on the 16th century when humanistic ideas of the Renaissance had a great impact on culture. At the same time professional art was influenced more and more by folk world outlook. Simplified images, decorative character, and the sincerity of disposition created the distinctive Ukrainian icon of that time.

128
The icon The Virgin of Volyn. 13th century

129
The icon St. George the Dragon Fighter. Early 16th century

130
Portrait of Mykhal Pototsky. By Miris

131
Portrait of Victoria Pocei. By F. Pavlikovych

West
Т. Шевченко

Landscape and portrait painting and still life were conceived concurrently with icon painting. Portraits were meant to glorify representatives of new Ukrainian gentry, Cossack chiefs, and well-to-do townsfolk. The Ukrainian gala portrait combined the traditions of monumental religious painting, West-European representative portrait, and the features of the Polish Sarmatian portrait. The famous artists and icon painters of the period were Mykola Petrakhnovych, Vasyl Petranovych, Yuriy Shymonovych, Stefan Dzenhalovych, celibate priest Samuil and others.

In the 17th–18th century baroque became a wide-spread trend in Ukrainian and European art as a whole. In Ukraine it is closely linked with traditional folk art. Such unification enriched the art of icon painting with festive mood and splended colour on the one hand, and toned down the exaltation of images characteristic of Catholic baroque on the other hand. Icon painting acquired secular colouring. The artists began to use chiaroscuro, the principles of spatial and aerial perspective, oil painting became more and more popular. Local schools such as Lviv painting guild, studios at Kyiv-Pechersk and Pochaiv Lvras, monasteries and noblemen's estates played a very important role at that time.

The late 18th–early 19th centuries in Ukraine proved a boundary that divided religious and secular art. This time is marked by the creative work of such outstanding portrait painters as Dmytro Levytsky and Volodymyr Borovykovsky who made Ukrainian art world-famous.

In the 19th century Petersburg Academy of Arts opened its doors for Ukrainian artists. At that time it was the only educational institution of higher learning that prepared professional artists according to European standards.

Ukrainian art of the middle of the 19th century is closely associated with the name of Taras Shevchenko. A former serf, pupil of Karl Brüllov, and member of Petersburg Academy of Art (engraving class), he consolidated the principles of realism in his creative work. His was an original and interesting idea of creating the album *Picturesque Ukraine* devoted to the history, monuments, life and nature of the native land.

The poetic and artistic images of Ukraine created by Shevchenko aroused people's interest in and love to their native country. His ideas inspired the artists Lev Zhemchuzhnikov, Ivan Sokolov, Kostiantyn Trutovsky.

The 19th century was the period of the establishment of the national school of landscape painting. At that time Ukraine was called East European Italy. Artists from the Russian Empire and other European countries visited Ukraine to enrich themselves with new themes and images. One of such artists was Vasyl Schternberg, a friend of Shevchenko's, master of lyrical landscape.

132
Monument to Taras Shevchenko in Lviv

133
Portrait of Hanna Zakrevska. By T. Shevchenko

134
Portrait of Borys Tomara. By H. Vasko

135
Portrait of the burgomaster of Poltava. By V. Borovykovsky.

136
Water-mill. By V. Shternberg.

137
Landscape. By H. Narbut.

138
Still-life. By A. Manevich.

Odesa art school and Kyiv drawing school occupied an important place at the beginning of the 20th century. Outstanding artists and pedagogues such as Mykola Murashko, Mykola Pymonenko, Ivan Selezniov taught in Kyiv school, frequent visiting teachers were Mikhail Vrubel, Vasiliy Vasnetsov, Illia Repin, Nikolai Ghe.

Ukrainian art of the turn of the 20th century could not avoid the influence of the leading European art trends — impressionism and post-impressionism, art nouveau, and various avant-garde tendencies.

The Ukrainian avant-garde of 1910–1930 is an interesting and extraordinary phenomenon represented by artists of extremely different trends.

Kharkiv school, where artists were under the influence of constructivism, was notable for its originality. It was represented by Anatol Petrytsky and Vasyl Yermylo. The latter can be considered father of the Ukrainian school of design. Oleksandra Ekster, a well-known reformer of theatrical art, propagated the ideas of cubiform futurism in painting, and worked in Kyiv. Among well-known artists of that period mention should be made of the ideologist of art, the author of the treatise *Painting and its Elements* Oleksandr Bohomazov, and David Burliuk

who had a bent for cubiform futurism like Oleksandra Ekster. Universally renowned Kazimir Malevich also had Ukrainian roots and often spoke of the influence of Ukrainian baroque and icon painting on his work. An original phenomenon of the early 20th century was Mykhailo Boychuk Art School. It strived to create national monumental art on the principles of religion, uniting it with the traditions of folk picture, local primitive painting and cheap popular print. Unfortunately, most of these artists were subjected to repression in the 1930s.

139
The Bridge. By O. Ekster

140
Three Ages. By F. Kkrychevsky

141
A Town. By S. Rybak

Ukrainian art of the Soviet period is represented by many talented and even unique painters, in spite of the difficult conditions of existence and self-expression. They are such luminaries of Ukrainian art as Heorhiy Melikhov, Oleksiy Budnykov, Viktor Kostetsky, Tetiana Yablonska, Oleksandr Shovkunenko, Oleksandr Lopukhov, Serhiy Hryhoriev and many others who preserved the best attainments of European realistic schools.

Western Ukrainian artists, who did not break relations with West-European painting schools till 1949, added a vivid page to the art of the post-war period. Ukrainian art of today is unimaginable without such names as F. Manaylo, A. Erdeli, Yosyp Bokshay, H. Hliuk, A. Kotska, R. Selsky, A Monastyrsky, K. Zvirynsky. This galaxy of masters reinterpreted the experience of Munich school, the formal searches of Czech neoprimitivists, and the achievements of neoimpressionism.

The 1960s (the time of the so-called Khruschev's thaw) enabled Ukrainian artists to familiarize themselves with the funds of world museums, with the contemporary art processes in Europe and America. This caused the emergence of various creative manners and trends. Tetiana Holembiyevska, M. Romanyshyn, O. Lopukhov and S. Shyshko continued to work in realistic manner, whereas Tetiana Yablonska, V. Volobuyev, V. Zaretsky and A. Horska immersed themselves in formalistic experiments.

Present-day Ukrainian art is developing in harmony with world art. National theme remains topical in painting — in thematic and historical pictures, in landscape, associative and formalistic works.

The 1990s were noted for the brave creative searches of various groups, including neo-figurative paintings of The Paris Commune (O. Holosiy), the elements of the formal painting language by members of the Painting Reserve (M. Heyko, A. Kryvolap, T. Silvashi, M. Kryvenko). Photographic art, video art and installations are developing at a rapid pace along with traditional painting. At the same time Ukrainian art remains an original and important component of Ukrainian culture as a whole.

142
Modern street painting

143
Art is eternal, and what is needed is body...

UR-NTB
148
АНТОНОВ
148
АНТОНОВ
UR-NTA

SCIENCE AND TECHNOLOGY

The most important achievements of Ukraine in the sphere of science and technology were linked with military industry. However, from the viewpoint of culture, training of personnel, the use of intellectual power, and influence on the scientific and technical environment, enterprises of the military-industrial complex made up only part of Ukrainian science and industry as a whole. Present-day heirs of the largest scientific-production complexes include enterprises of aircraft industry, rocket and space technology, shipbuilding, electric engineering, instrument-making, radio engineering, communication, information science, computer engineering techniques, machine building, power engineering, etc. Ukrainian aircraft-design centers have provided world technology with a series of inimitable solutions, particularly in the sphere of transport aircraft; these achievements belong to Antonov Design Bureau that was organized in Kyiv after the war.

The cosmic fate of Ukraine seems to have been favorable. Interest of the romantic youth in conquering outer space was realized in the works of scientists of the 1930s. Fate rescued the pioneer of rocket business *Oleksandr Sharhey* who lived under the name of *Yuriy Kondratiuk*. Written in Poltava in 1929 his work "Conquering of Interplanetary Space" was used by American scientists when they planned landing on the Moon, where on their initiative the name of the Ukrainian scientist was immortalized.

Odesa resident *V. P. Hlushko* created a series of rocket engines as long ago as the early 1930s. *S. P. Koroliov*, an outstanding Ukrainian aircraft designer, contributed a great deal to the conquering of outer space by the Soviet Union in the late 1950s–early 1960s. The Special Design Bureau "Pivdenne" headed by *M. K. Yanhel* created strategic rockets and, on their basis, man-made satellites of the Earth "Kosmos," "Tsyklon" and "Zenit."

In fact atomic power engineering became a by-product of the military industry. Nuclear power-plants for sub-marines worked out by *A. P. Aleksandrov* were used at most of the nuclear power stations in Ukraine built after 1971–1975. The inexorable course of the history of nuclear energy that led to Chornobyl tragedy clearly revealed shortcomings in the principles upon which scientific and technical progress was based in totalitarian and post-totalitarian society.

It is only natural that scientific and technical achievements connected with the military industry represented only the kernel of industrial culture. Thousands of geologists, mining engineers, metallurgists, bridge-builders, power engineering specialists and many others worked and continue to work in Ukraine. Ukrainian scientists and engineers have gained great achievements in the field of material engineering, particularly in electric welding, powder metallurgy, artificial diamonds production and instruments for them. Ukrainian scientific centers were connected with the most advanced branches of the fundamental sciences concerning the World. Kyiv has become an acknowledged international center of non-linearity and turbulence theory in which new methods of approach to microcosm and cosmology physics have been formed.

During the 20th century Ukraine made a great leap in the field of education, science and technology. As of today Ukraine is one of the four leading states in the sphere of space technology (along with USA, Russia and China). Ukraine with its population of nearly 50 million represents tremendous possibilities of civilization progress. Its well-trained specialists, lucid minds and clever fingers make Ukraine a world of boundless possibilities.

144
Test-flight of AN-148

145
AN-225 being loaded in Kabul

146
Cosmonautics Museum in Zhytomyr

ATHENS 2004

SPORT

Sport life of the country is a special phenomenon. And it is not only because Ukrainian athletes are well known throughout the world, but because the beginnings of such fame lie in the natural talent of the nation that can be compared perhaps with its fondness and knack of singing. Football (soccer) is the most popular game in Ukraine. The lion's share of success in this kind of sports belongs to the club "Dynamo" Kyiv that started its history in 1924.

The team of the capital city of Soviet Ukraine became the most titled team in the higher league of the USSR, having won the title of the champions of the country 13 times. "Dynamo" twice won the title of the European Cup Holders' Cup, and once the title of the UEFA Supercup Holders (1975). This success is associated primarily with the name of the legendary football player and coach Valeriy Lobanovsky; three of his players — Oleg Blokhin, Ihor Belanov and Andriy Shevchenko — became "Golden Ball" winners. During Ukraine's independence little has changed — Kyivites continue victorious traditions having been the champions of Ukraine 11 times, and receiving the cherished star on their uniform.

However, while speaking of Ukrainian football it would not be correct to mention only one team — there are a number of serious representatives on the continental arena besides 'Dynamo" Kyiv. It is first of all "Shakhtar" Donetsk and "Dnipro" Dnipropetrovsk. Lately the Ukrainian national has performed with confidence as well. A further important step in the development of football will be the European championship — 2012.

The world-famous Ukrainian women's handball club "Spartak" won the title of the USSR champion 20 years running, and 13 times came out the winner in the European Champions' Cup tournament. These victories are connected with the name of another outstanding coach — Ihor Turchin. His wife Zinaida Turchina was recognized the best handballer of the 20th century. Today there is also a galaxy of talented sportswomen who won bronze medals at the Olympiad in Athens, gaining the upper hand over the French national, the current world champion.

The State gives much consideration to single combat sports; to innumerate all the Ukrainian stars in these kinds of sports is practically impossible. The names of the boxers Vitaliy and Volodymyr Klichko do not disappear from the pages of the Ukrainian and foreign press.

The Ukrainian swimmer Yana Klochkova is the only one in history of the Olympic Games who won two gold medals (200 m and 400 m) at two Olympiads in succession.

The alumni of Albina and Iryna Deriuhina Callisthenics School give a great deal of trouble to their rivals. They have been legisla-

147
Yana Klochkova – a swimming superstar

148
Andriy Shevchenko, a favorite of football fans

WORLD
CHAMPION
WBC

tors in this kind of sport for many years. Not long ago Oleksandra Tymoshenko and Kateryna Serebrianska celebrated their victories, and today Bessonova and Natalia Hudenko continue to prove the high class of Ukrainian callisthenics. The programs of our girls are really creations of art that spectators watch with bated breath.

Ukraine's gymnasts, representatives of one of the oldest kinds of sport, do not lag behind others. Victorious traditions in this sport were laid by the many-time Olympic champions Larysa Latynina (9 gold medals) and Borys Shakhlin (7 gold medals). Due to these outstanding athletes the fame of Ukrainian gymnastics resounded all over the world; Valeriy Goncharov was the last to win "gold" in Athens.

Wrestling is a well-developed sport in Ukraine. Elbrus Tedeyev and Iryna Merleni won the highest awards at the Olympiad in Athens. The 12th team place in Athens is not a bad index for a young State.

Ukraine has achieved success not only in summer kinds of sports. It has a galaxy of talented sportsmen in winter sports. They are primarily figure skaters Olena Hrushyna and Ruslan Honcharov who won bronze medals at the last world championship. Oksana Bayul (ladies singles) became gold medallist in Lillehamer in 1994.

Climate in Ukraine is not quite suitable for winter kinds of sports, but our biathlonists, tobogganers, and free style skiers train not only abroad; necessary conditions have been created for them in the Carpathian Mountains in Ukraine.

149
Vitaliy and Volodymyr Klychko, a legend of boxing

150
Hanna Bessonova, a star of Ukrainian calisthenics

CONTENTS

General Information 5
Historical Events 6
Nature 9
Parks and Reserves 19
Architecture 35
Language 47
Old Beliefs 51
Folk Holidays and Rites 55
Folk Culture 59
Traditional Cuisine 73
Professional Culture 79
Science and Technology 95
Sport 97

UKRAINE

Photograph album

Reviewed by *Myroslav Popovych*

Written by *Oleksandr Bilousko*
Translated from the Ukrainian by *Viktor Kotolupov*

Photographs by
Yuriy Buslenko, Andriy Denyskiv, Yevhen Derlemenko, Sviatoslav Kolesnykov, Ihor Kropyvnytsky, Andriy Sovenko, Kostiantyn Starodub, Viktor Khmara, Oleksandr Chaptsev

Director general *Rūta Malikenaite*
Editor-in-Chief *Wirginijus Strolia*
Executive editor *Olena Kiryatska*
Layout and design by *Vitaliy Mashkov*
Prepared for printing by *Ihor Artemenko*

Baltia Druk Publishers,
51/2 A. Barbusse St., Kyiv, Ukraine, 03150
Tel. +38(044)502 1047; e-mail: *info@baltia.com.ua*; *www.baltia.com.ua*

ISBN 966-8137-20-5